Praise

'Forget the fairy tales. Ben Hughes, an exceptional talent, delivers the unvarnished truth about building a sustainable music career. This book is the pragmatic, battle-tested guide the industry desperately needs, written by someone who walks the walk.'
 — **Bernie Hollywood OBE JP**, global charity chair and governance architect

'I wish I had access to this kind of information when I was starting out in the industry. From a scan through Ben's book, I could have easily picked up points that are only obvious to me now after twenty years in the game.'
 — **Dan Dare**, artist, songwriter and producer

'Whether you're just starting out or a fully fledged member of this brutal, beautiful industry, this is a must-read. Every musical education establishment should have this book available on their shelves for all students to pour over. Ben manages to explain every element of the industry with full candour yet no bitterness, glowing over its high points and making clear the pitfalls, while heralding the golden moments. I wish I'd had this book when I was eighteen.'
 — **Lorna Blackwood**, vocal coach

'Brilliant – this book is honest, frank and full of advice that every new starter needs to know!'
 — **Gyasi Sheppy**, television presenter, Ceebeebies!

'Everyone who is in music or wants to be in music should read this book. It not only applies to the music industry but has some top tips for life – all-round solid advice.'
 — **Sam Handley**, sales development lead, MM Band Services

'A great read. This book presents everything in a highly readable, systematic approach to the development of the craft and gives you a broad perspective on other considerations needed to progress.'
 — **Simon Duffy**, artist manager, Tri-Tone

'Ben writes this book with the same care that he shows in person: protective, empathetic and always urging young musicians to find success on their own terms.'
 — **Jacq Burns**, literary agent

make music your business

the musician's
blueprint
for a
thriving career

ben hughes

Rethink

First published in Great Britain in 2025 by Rethink Press (www.rethinkpress.com)

© Copyright Ben Hughes

All rights reserved. No part of this publication may be reproduced, stored in or introduced into a retrieval system, or transmitted, in any form, or by any means (electronic, mechanical, photocopying, recording or otherwise) without the prior written permission of the publisher.

The right of Ben Hughes to be identified as the author of this work has been asserted by him in accordance with the Copyright, Designs and Patents Act 1988.

This book is sold subject to the condition that it shall not, by way of trade or otherwise, be lent, resold, hired out, or otherwise circulated without the publisher's prior consent in any form of binding or cover other than that in which it is published and without a similar condition including this condition being imposed on the subsequent purchaser.

Cover image © Shutterstock | Manovector

Contents

Introduction   **1**

1 Know Your History   **7**
    How the industry has evolved   8
    The new rhythm   10
    Who are you?   12
    What's your plan?   13

2 Stay True To Your Message   **17**
    Keeping things in perspective   18
    Trusting your intuition   21
    Why your message is important   23
    How to create your message   29

3 Make Music   **37**
    What is born talent?   38
    Making yourself good at music   39

A sliding scale 41
What matters most 44
Creating a good workflow 46

4 Explore Your Craft 53
What is the song for? 53
Smashing things together to create something new 56
Keeping this simple 61
The recording and production process 64
The importance of co-writes 68
Getting the word out 71

5 Perform Live 75
Putting on a show 79
Improvising and hustling 83
The value of the small venue 89
Enhancing your live performance 93

6 Grow Your Community And Scale It Up 97
Embracing social media 97
Making social media work for you 103
Breaking some myths and maximising engagement 106
The phases of marketing 110

7	**Get A Team**	**121**
	Why you need a team	123
	How to create a team	126
	How to choose your manager	140
8	**Make Plans**	**147**
	Money talks	149
	Stating your terms	151
	Management plans	153
	Getting your team aligned with your message	155
	Collaborating with PR	157
	Keeping your head in the right place	159
9	**Be Resilient**	**165**
	Resilience is about being flexible	169
	You need to learn to say no	171
	Discipline creates tunnel vision	173
	Handling rejection	179
	Diversifying your income	182
	The power of financial health	184
10	**Craft Your Story**	**191**
	The direction of your story	191
	The message vs the story	193

The tenets of storytelling in music	198
Don't just chase the money!	202
Conclusion	**207**
Say Hello	**209**
Notes	**211**
Acknowledgements	**213**
The Author	**217**

Introduction

If you want success in the music industry, I want to ask you something: Are you doing what it takes to be good at your craft?

At the outset, you might have conceived of a pre-destined career in the music industry because you discovered your best singing voice in the privacy of your shower, or because you've entertained friends at a birthday gathering or a karaoke bar. Maybe you're further ahead than this now. It could be that you're already gigging, starting to get people coming to your shows, and having people liking your TikToks. Are these things enough to succeed and sustain you as an artist in the music business, though? In simple terms, the answer is no.

While talent and practice are undoubtedly essential, they only form the raw materials of what is a viable career. The challenge lies in the common misconception that singing a catchy tune at a karaoke, or even having a sold-out show in your hometown filled with your friends and family, automatically equates to genuine talent and indicates an inevitable path to lucrative record deals. The reality is much more complex and capricious, and it demands a lot more.

If you happen to know people in the music industry, that's a great start. You're bound to enjoy some success if your dad is the president of Warner Brothers, or if you're best friends with Billie Eilish or Bastille. If you have a friend who works closely with a big agent or a great manager, obviously that's a great start and things will happen. For the rest of us, we are very much on our own. If that includes you, you need a plan.

Getting started in the music industry is the same as setting up a business, complete with all the implications that come with it. Everyone from the artists through to the top-level record executives has their sights set on turning a profit. Nobody has a crystal ball to be able to predict the future, so the sustainability of the whole industry hinges on it being viable for everyone along the journey.

Industries are fundamentally rooted in economics, and they must function in a way that benefits their

INTRODUCTION

participants. For the same reason no one would place a substantial bet on a horse in a national race unless they believed it had a real chance, every facet of the music industry is about making yourself the winning horse.

Factors such as government regulations, inflation rates, the cost of living, consumer preferences, mass psychology and technological advancements can significantly influence the dynamics and progression of the music industry. It is essential for individuals like officials and investors, as well as aspiring creators and hopeful entrepreneurs, to grasp the workings of it if they're to have a chance of getting in and out the industry unscathed. Like in a game of chess, there's no guaranteed outcome, but the more you understand, the better you are equipped, and the better chess player you become.

So what does the music industry want from you?

While mastering fundamental skills like technique and musical processes is a good yardstick, they are not necessarily the factors that count the most. Just because you're technically a good musician, that doesn't necessarily guarantee the work will come your way. What truly distinguishes exceptional musicians, especially the successful ones, are qualities beyond their musical knowledge and ability. These additional strengths might be called luck by many people, but the simple truth is that if you make a solid

3

plan, you can create your own luck. This book will help you develop new habits and values that will allow you to grasp the bigger picture and to make a lifechanging plan for achieving success in the music industry. The principles within these pages are applicable to all aspiring artists.

To stand out in this context means reaching a level of excellence and cultivating a unique identity that sets you apart from the rest. My ultimate aim is to empower you to take greater control of your music career while maintaining a grounded perspective, no matter where you are in the industry.

Some people think that all they need is extraordinary talent, and then some fairy-godmother figure will magically discover and sign them. Success comes, though, from a combination of both the love and the economics of the situation that make it click. Nowadays there's a much more rigorous process by which artists are 'vetted' by the industry, and the ways that fans find and appreciate artists has also evolved a great deal. A band being signed on pure optimism is now extremely rare, even though that used to be more common.

Most important is to first know your own mind. In the chapters of this book, I'll share what I consider to be ten crucial points that will help you along the way:

1. Know your history
2. Stay true to your message

3. Make music

4. Explore your craft

5. Perform live

6. Grow your community and scale it up

7. Get a team

8. Make plans

9. Be resilient

10. Craft your story

Understanding what truly drives you reveals the path of how to get it. Throughout this book we'll explore success from all angles. We'll bring in music, psychology and philosophy, and stories from people who've chased their dreams and made them happen. You simply have to decide on what needs to be done and *do* it. You can't rely on being discovered in the privacy of your bedroom.

In the quest for personal growth and transformation, the importance of mindset cannot be overstated. Our mindset shapes our perceptions, influences our actions and, ultimately, determines the course of our lives. For me the end game isn't confined to a monochromatic version of success, and it never has been. It is about getting a deeper sense of life through creativity and through working hard at something, and in enjoying the journey, however that journey pans out.

The quest for a career in music, a great band and a happy life is in your own journey, and genuine understanding can only happen when you're amongst it, in the thick of it, trying things out and being willing to get some things wrong. If music is life, then the least we can do is play a decent tune.

As you're reading, keep the ideas that are useful to you and discard the rest. Keep a notebook handy to record any relevant points and to highlight the bits that leave the biggest impression on you.

ONE
Know Your History

The best place to start is where you are. What do you already know about the music industry? For most people the music business appears to work on a cocktail of smoke, mirrors, sex, drugs and huge amounts of luck. This is only partially true.

Just as it pays to study a map before going off exploring, it's useful to start your new journey by understanding the reason the music industry currently is the way it is. This chapter outlines a brief history of the industry and why it is useful for us to know that.

How the industry has evolved

Back in the 1960s and through to the 1980s, two crucial things were happening:

1. This was a completely different time from today, during which there were rapid technological advancements in music.

2. These advancements shaped not only the minds of the people making music but also the minds of the ordinary fans listening to that music.

Record companies had a lot of money to invest in different types of talents. New recording methods and new instruments like synthesisers were developed, which amazed people around the world. Exciting and fresh sounds captivated the creators and consumers alike. Imagine how things were when bands like The Shadows, with their clean guitar tones, were the norm; and then Jimi Hendrix exploded on the scene, setting his guitar on fire on stage, distorting amps and sounding like he'd done a deal with the Devil. Everyone must've shit themselves!

Think about the humungous shock it must've been, when all that people were used to listening to was a Django Reinhardt recording, achieved by just putting a mic in a room with three or four guys. Then suddenly The Beatles burst onto the scene, with full stereo mixes featuring reverse guitars, wild noises, sitars, distorted amps, and mental arrangements like 'I Am the Walrus'. Pioneers were everywhere, exploring and creating unique inventions and fresh sounds, the wilder and more unorthodox the better. Some artists were writing songs ten minutes long, weaving rock and opera into the same genre. It's no surprise that artists like David Bowie, Kate Bush, Steely Dan, Pink Floyd, Diana Ross, Joni Mitchell, Yes, Genesis and other progressives in the 1970s emerged out of this amazing period. It wouldn't have been out of place to see a Marshall stack welded to a rabbit hutch, while microphones whirled around a ceiling fan to get that special sound. (If you don't know all the artists above, look 'em up! You don't necessarily have to like them, but who knows – you could stumble on something you really like.)

It's so easy to see why everyone's minds were flipped by this abundance of recorded creativity. There's a marked distinction too – the scene was as tough as it still is today, but success was riding mainly on artists' music rather than on their social media and their talent for persona. The other crucial technological difference between then and now emerged through the birth, existence and now global takeover of the internet. Back in the day, discovering this raw, new and genuinely groundbreaking talent in the local bars was not only super-exciting; it was also the *only* way to keep up with the industry on the ground. Cut to today, and this is simply not the case, for both good and bad reasons.

The new rhythm

The internet has changed not only the way we listen to music but also the way we *think* about music. The whole structure of the way society listens to and buys music is not what it was. Our attention span has significantly dropped, and now we're obsessed with money and sex in a much stranger and ever more confusing way than ever before. In a world where these things are expedient commodities, music is no longer a pioneering adventure, aiming to alter the course of history. It's not a carefully put-together meal like a roast dinner; instead it functions much more like penny sweets, quickly bought, consumed and discarded.

Once the mission of music was as follows:

- Capture the hearts and minds of the fans that turn up to your concerts
- Make a statement
- Put on a great show, exploring your creative boundaries to push limits

Now the objectives appear to be:

- Appeal to the widest audience possible (which is now the world)
- As quickly as possible, grab instantaneous attention by any and all means at your disposal

- Don't get hung up on any single idea
- Always keep moving on to the next thing

The way we now consume music in the mainstream is *fast, fast, fast*. Music has to explode in the first three seconds of a TikTok video to grab anyone's attention, and it needs to show sex appeal in a big way. That means songs have begun to sound a particular way; the choruses have to do certain, set things; and each musician has to be a personality in their own right, with all the bells and whistles. Musicians are everything from gym bunnies, drag queens and comedians to political activists, scientists, clergy, postmen, wrestlers – you name it. The Pink Floyd album *Dark Side of the Moon* would never be made in today's economy. The first track, 'Breathe', has a slow tempo, with the lyrics not kicking in until one minute twenty seconds. Most TikTok videos are viewed, liked, subscribed, shared, and watched again in the space of ten seconds!

Creatively, this now means that progressive music is rarer. It also means that your traditional A&R (artists and repertoire) 'man' isn't seeking the same things he was back in the day. He would've been hanging out in bars listening to every bizarre chord and wacky gizmo. Now he hangs out in Starbucks, combing through TikTok, Spotify, SoundCloud and every other social profile, looking for stats, and listening to young teenagers to find out what they're into and who has the most wide-ranging appeal. Based on that alone, by the time he's ordered one latte, he's probably looked at your numbers and decided he's not into you. He touches base with the live scene *only* when he's confident that an artist's stats and metrics – streaming numbers, ticket and record sales, chart positions, etc – match up to the real world out there.

Sounds cynical, right? Sorry, folks, but don't shoot the messenger – that's the state of play today. Don't panic, though. First, you knowing all this means that your attitude going into it will be different. You need to know where the industry is, because that tells you where it's going. It's a new landscape, yes, but that doesn't mean it's impossible to navigate that landscape or to be creative.

Instead of thinking, *I must impress the whole world with my instantly likeable Instagram videos*, artists everywhere are now going the other way.

They are saying, *I will impress my small community of thirty followers and hope to grow them over time…* and it's working.

Who are you?

In a world where a million people have great 'stats', I think it's important to recognise first the need for letting go of your own entitlement. Why should *you* be the one to succeed? Why should anyone listen to *you*, when other people may be funnier, prettier, sexier, smarter, and so on? Also, what is it *exactly* that you have to offer?

This gives you your starting point: What is everyone else doing, so you can do something different?

The fact is the public now want to know you first and your music second. While it might seem a good idea to pretend to be someone else to make it big, or to pay people for inflated Spotify or socials numbers, audiences can see through that act. It's not stats or money or A&R people that make great artists. Being genuine and true to yourself is what really connects with fans, builds your community, makes you authentic, and makes fans feel something and remain loyal. In this gluttonous and perverse world of sex and money, people want realness. They want an oasis away from all the fancy meetings, the Botox and the boring company suits with great Instagram numbers. They want to know *you*.

What's your plan?

In trying to make it, you'll unquestionably encounter countless people who will bombard you with all sorts of recommendations, and amidst that sea of advice, their explanations and methodologies all start to blend together. In this day and age, advice on how to make it big in the music industry is as abundant as the fish in the sea. You've got people blabbering about success in courses and college degrees. You'll hear from everyone, from self-proclaimed gurus to A-list celebrities. They'll all have their two cents to say to an aspiring artist, and they'll all want to offer *their* way to get there. The best thing you can do is to tell them all to fuck off until you've thought about your plan.

What is certain is that absolutely nobody can predict the future. There are, however, valuable indicators, strategies, trends and maxims that offer a much better chance of success than you crossing your fingers and toes, making a random guess, and praying somebody scoops you up and lands you in the big bucks.

Why certain songs become hits while others fade away isn't an exact science, but it shares similarities with predicting the weather. There are indicators and trends that, when combined, can lead to a fairly accurate forecast to tell you that a storm is coming, though it can never be guaranteed.

I've seen how those who've been offered shortcuts to success through bad advice, where they're promised the world in exchange for no effort, no fanbase, and no quality music, usually see their projects crash within the first three to six months. Through my own journey, I've learned that you have to play the long game. You've got to commit to a process. Whether you're talking to a high-powered record executive in LA or a humble music teacher in Sheffield, both can offer valuable insights, but neither has the ability to give you a foolproof path. Ultimately, everything has to come from within you, and only you can choose to stay the course and stick to a plan.

TRY THIS NOW: Subjective advice

Go and ask two completely different musicians a question about how to learn and play an Arctic Monkeys song.

Wherever you've decided to make notes on this book, write down what those two musicians said.

I'm willing to bet that both people will have laid out distinct ideas and given you quite different advice on how to tackle the same challenge.

Although the goal is the same, the outcome will be largely dependent on your own personality, the way you best take in information, and the kind of person you are in terms of acting on that advice.

It is key to know yourself and to get your strategy in place for the long game. Independent labels and major labels all look for certain things. Their shopping list includes:

- Some promising social media stats
- A dedicated fan base that pays money to attend your shows and actively engages online
- A solid, thirty-minute live performance

- The right equipment, and transportation to pull it off

- An EP of recorded material with more waiting in the wings

- A person that's likeable and easy to get on with

- The ability to continually generate new content

- Some experience in making demos, using software like GarageBand or Logic Pro X

On top of all that, you'll probably need to have set about releasing music through a distributor and started connecting with the online music community. That's right – any serious label wants all this before they'll even think about leaving Starbucks to see you!

Young artists, take note: the game has changed. It's no longer only about the music; it's about being a self-sufficient, well-rounded individual. You have to become a well-oiled machine that can fit into an even bigger machine that may decide to get involved. If you're not fulfilling those factors, there are plenty more people who will be. Always remember: there's someone out there right now who's working harder, getting smarter and doing everything you're trying to do.

TWO
Stay True To Your Message

Understanding and defining yourself is key. When you clearly know who you are and the core message behind your philosophy, then everything about your project or your music naturally falls into place. This chapter explores the value of a core message and how to create one.

Honing your message is all about getting to the bottom of your motivations for striving for success in the music industry. If you're simply looking to have some fun, you need not read any further. If you're trying, though, to cultivate something and craft a career, especially a career in the limelight, it pays to keep yourself in check.

Keeping things in perspective

Striving for the ultimate goals of being signed, becoming famous and getting lots of money has the unfortunate capacity of distorting a person's ego. If unchecked at the beginning, this can lead to some unbalanced behaviour later on. How do you take care of yourself in such an unpredictable industry? How do you maintain your motivation for continuous content creation, staying on top of trends, nurturing creativity, and constantly exploring new forms of self-expression?

Just like other essential qualities, humility is something to practise not only onstage but also in your everyday life. Humility is borne out of love – the love you have for what you do: the live performances, the music you're crafting, and the connection with your audience.

When people become obsessed with reaching the peak of success, like getting a record deal or topping the charts, it messes them up and all too often destroys them and their relationships with others. There are those amongst us who have zero idea of how to succeed other than by bulldozing over anybody and everybody to get to the top. Those people eventually abuse the privileges they've gained because they start to see those privileges as entitlements, and even those supposed entitlements are never enough for them. There is no denying that there are a lot of successful but corrupt people in the music industry.

The sad truth is that we look up to people who've made it, believing they are in a position to shape our idea of success and tell us how to achieve it. They often hold the keys and tempt us with promises. They say that others can make it in the music industry by doing exactly what they say. The most vulnerable among us, especially young people, often fall for it completely. They're blinded by the bright lights of fame and glory, failing to see the more manipulative and harder realities. When success is pursued without considering its full context, individuals are often willing to trample over innocent people; while others, in their blind pursuit of fame and money, are trampled on.

To become successful, you need to manage your energy and understand where you're really at. This can often feel like a constant battle, trying to please others and having to make compromises. Over the years, in the quest for money and famous encounters, I've personally missed countless important occasions – birthdays, celebrations and reunions with others. I often question the value of those choices.

Pursuing success and finding happiness from it is of no use whatsoever when that 'success' is confined to an ashram or yoga studio, or a million-dollar tour bus. It must work for you in the daily grind, even when life is at its very worst. Your mind must be content to do the work when you don't have the money for the rent, when your career isn't quite going the way you want it to, or when you're in the grips of panic because your label dropped you or your drum kit got crushed in an elevator. Success has to be a living, breathing reality. Otherwise, it may be marvellous poetry, but it will be of no actual use.

I'd bet there are teenagers out there right now, feeling genuine anxiety and relying on medication because they haven't received BRIT Awards. This is not an overexaggeration. Given the enormity and the power of the web and the prestige of celebrity status, it's understandable that young, aspiring musicians can get swept up in the allure and supposed glamour of everything they see, and why many sadly end up losing themselves in the process.

If you look beyond yourself for success, you will be lost. The notion of a 'purpose' predetermined by fate is nothing more than an illusion – a distraction created by fraudsters and TV shows. You're not 'destined' to be a success in the music industry; there's only those who work at it, and those who don't. Similarly, if you only look to other people, and buy into the idea of an *X Factor* judge or a similar gatekeeper telling you where your career is going or how your creativity should look, then you will still be lost, because people won't notice you because of how well you take instructions (whether from fate, the gods or Simon Cowell); they take notice of who you are, what you do and what you have to say. Opportunities for careers, wealth and fame tend to come your way naturally when you genuinely lead the way, not when you wait for some gatekeeper to will it. They come when you know who you are, what your message is and what your story is, and when you can see clearly what you can do in the world.

Trusting your intuition

Someone will tell you it's right to get a music deal in such a way, or they'll tell you the correct way to write a song. Some people will tell you that you have to get a degree in music, while others will say it's imperative you leave education at all costs. Someone will tell you that you have to make this or that decision, or vote Democrat, or play a G Major. The truth is that any of those advice givers may be right or wrong, but you'll never be able to work that out before you know your own mind.

The best teachers out there are the ones that make you not need teachings. Simply put, you're far better off learning about your industry, playing the long game and committing to hard graft with a plan than simply saying yes to everyone. You have to actually go and do it. By doing something – anything at all – you're already on your way to making things happen and quitting all that internal monologue about doing 'the right thing'.

Love, passion and community are what make work meaningful. They bring you closer to others and to something bigger than yourself. Students often ask me about how to open doors. My honest response is that they should knock once; and if they don't get an answer, so what?

Trust in what you're doing, and you could soon realise that the door you truly need to open is to something entirely different. Ultimately, what I'm still learning is that you can spend so much time working to open doors to advance your career, but you just might not be able to. You can bang away on doors for a lifetime, and some of them remain firmly shut, sometimes for reasons you'll never even know.

TRY THIS NOW: Realistic goals

Think of the thing you want to do or be most in the world, and write down your goal.

Recognise right at the start of your journey that you don't need individuals in your life who don't support you. You don't need a mindset that beats you up, and you shouldn't invite anything into your life that hinders you. It's crucial to be honest with yourself from the beginning.

Thinking about your goal, consider what you would be prepared to commit to – how many hours and how much money.

Make notes on whether you would be willing to keep striving for your goal if you knew it was going to require years of hard work. Would you still be as driven two to five years from now?

Why your message is important

Your message is important because it:

- Provides you with stability and consistency for your goals
- Communicates a clear philosophy for everything you do

Making a message is *not* about creating some abstract, introspective waffle that makes you internally aware but completely clueless about the business. On the contrary, a message is a genuine necessity for building your band, your music, your persona and everything else that comes later.

Many artists initially look outside of themselves to define their identity. They are influenced by social media, famous figures and Hollywood trends. They see the glitz and glamour of festivals, talk shows and media exposure, which makes them believe they must conform to an industry-pleasing version of themselves. This is a fatal mistake that sabotages careers before they even begin.

You shouldn't begin by saying, for example: *I want 20 million followers and to play Coachella by the end of the year.*

You should begin by asking yourself: *What am I good at, and what can I do?*

There are three main reasons for this:

1. Change
2. Consistency
3. Pressure

1. Change

The music industry is constantly evolving. You are a drop in a sea of aspiring talents, all vying for attention in an ever-changing landscape. Trying to keep up with trends as well as shouting the loudest in the din of millions of other talented people would quickly drain your resources and lead to financial ruin within a short span. Imagine you decide to make a music video with 1980s hairstyles, say. You shoot it, and it costs you an arm and a leg. Then by the time you've paid for it, edited it, got it ready for release and put it out there, the industry has already moved on to Mods, Emos or 1990s Oasis lookalikes in parka jackets. If you wanted to keep up with the industry, you'd have to keep reshooting your video, updating your style every time, and you'd be financially bankrupt within six months.

2. Consistency

Altering your image or brand too frequently causes a lack of consistency for fans, who may struggle to grasp your true identity. When fans are uncertain about whether the musician is a folk artist or a country pop singer, say, they can't fully support and connect with the artist or what their music stands for and sounds like.

3. Pressure

Frequent style and brand changes create mental turmoil. You'll find yourself playing constant mind games to stay relevant, have the right platform, have the right number of followers, dress correctly, say the right things, sound the right way, and so on. The pressure to keep pace with industry trends often leads to crippling financial strains and feelings of failure when expected success doesn't materialise.

The bottom line is that you need to avoid paying undue attention to trends and external influences when defining yourself as an artist. Instead, focus on shutting out the noise, listening to your inner voice and having unwavering belief in your music and your artistic vision. Stay true to yourself, and see your journey through with determination and authenticity.

Although this approach may appear straightforward or obvious, many people shy away from doing it or don't think it's all that important. However, it is the most vital step. Self-awareness serves as the bedrock for surmounting all the challenges the music industry can throw at you. A spider catches its prey just as effectively as a cheetah. It doesn't matter in the beginning whether your strategy is to wait or charge, or whether you spend or save. The key is in finding what you're distinctive at and fully embracing it.

Always avoid the temptation of conforming to others or comparing yourself with them. Instead, celebrate what sets you apart and makes you special. Allow your values to guide you, and set meaningful goals as you shape your identity moving forward. Surround yourself with supportive individuals who encourage your growth and positivity as you work on defining who you are. Embrace your imperfections, because they are the very thing that create your individuality.

Mike Walker: The sound of truth

In 2005, at the Liverpool Institute for Performing Arts, I met Mike Walker, a musician whose journey and approach to music would go on to shape my own understanding of authenticity in art.

Mike isn't just any musician. He's a guitarist, composer, teacher and counsellor; and he's an expert in the art of improvisation, which he views as instant composition. His music – a blend of jazz, rock, funk, folk and everything in between – reflects his versatility and depth. What struck me most about Mike, though, is how deeply he connects with music and how that connection defines his life.

Growing up, Mike wasn't always drawn to music. In school maths tests he was more focused on drawing strange animal hybrids than anything else. At that time he didn't dream of becoming a musician. Inspired by a movie, he instead wanted to be a werewolf, but things changed when he was around sixteen years old. His brother played music, and Mike was captivated by the way he could sing while playing the guitar. Inspired, Mike picked up the instrument himself, learning about alternate tunings from artists like Joni Mitchell.

It was through his sister that Mike discovered a world of diverse music, from Led Zeppelin's powerful riffs to the intricate soundscapes of Mahavishnu Orchestra. He found himself gravitating toward jazz, where he absorbed the sounds of Coltrane, Parker and Hall. Playing with his brother's bands and joining the jazz fusion group River People in Manchester exposed Mike to new creative avenues. Soon he was touring with legends like the Impossible Gentlemen, with musicians Steve Swallow and Adam Nussbaum, Gwilym Simcock and Nikki Iles.

Despite his many collaborations and achievements, including his own ambitious album *Madhouse and the Whole Thing There*, it's Mike's approach to the creative process that resonates most. He's a storyteller, not only through music but also through words, with a deep appreciation for how music can reflect one's true self. His album *The Things That Make The Darklings Sing*, which at the time of this book being published has been composed but not yet recorded, was inspired by the imagery in Keats's poetry, proving that even the most unconventional ideas could be the starting point for powerful artistic expression.

What makes Mike's journey so powerful is his unwavering commitment to authenticity. He says you need to 'mind your own nature, to not be afraid of that, and to move into your own life and write about you'.

Mike also advised that people shouldn't be a chameleon, trying to match what others are doing. Instead, they should look inside and ask themselves how they convey that moment of their life in sound.

For Mike music isn't about following a formula; it's about exploring and expressing what feels real to you, right now. It's a lesson that cuts across all creative fields, not only music. To truly make an impact, to truly resonate with others, you must first be true to yourself.

Mike's music, with its honest complexity, continues to inspire me to push past surface-level trends and dive deeper into the spaces that reflect my own experiences. If we approach our creativity with the same genuine curiosity, we can all find the sounds and stories that resonate most.

The full interview with Mike, filled with more insights into his unique approach to music and life, is a reminder that in music, as in life, authenticity is the key.

You can hear the interview on my *More in the Moni* podcast at www.moreinthemoni.com.

How to create your message

Once you see yourself as you truly are rather than how you wish to be, your personal message emerges naturally. Your message, in simple words, is a genuine expression of who you are. It should be like looking at a tree and describing it without embellishments, suppression, alteration or sales pitches – you're just stating what you see and how you feel.

This message becomes the spark that ignites curiosity in others, regardless of whether you have an effervescent personality or a more reserved one. Consider this message the heart and soul of your songwriting and performances, and later also of your marketing, your wardrobe, your social media account and everything else.

When we share our message with genuine honesty, something magical happens. We attract the people who truly want to listen and connect with us, and together, we create our own awesome community. If the message gets muddled, or if we haven't fully thought it through, everything can seem confusing and unclear to everyone involved.

Let's say you're all about conquering the world, but deep down, you're actually a shy person who doesn't want any fuss. That's gonna create some confusion in your message. Or imagine you're putting out a message of political dissent, but in reality, you're a law-abiding citizen through and through, who thinks paying taxes is a great idea. Again, it's gonna create confusion, and it'll seep into everything you do – your image, your songs, your style.

TRY THIS NOW: Crafting your message

Grab a pen and paper, and as you read the next pages, start to think about your own message and how to refine it.

As you do that, keep these questions clearly in your mind:

- What does my message mean to me?
- How does it connect with what's most important to me?

Here are some personal artistic messages or statements that might inspire you, and your own message could be similar to one or more of these:

- I think it's important to help others whenever I can.
- I believe that hard work always pays off.
- I believe in absolutely nothing, and the world needs changing.
- I believe in God.
- All I want is loads of sex and drugs.

- The only thing that matters in life is money.
- I come from a life of crime.
- I am a bored suburban housewife.
- I want to travel the world.
- I really suffer with my mental health.

The beauty is that there's no 'right' way to be. Your identity, appearance, actions and message are uniquely yours. There are no mistakes; there are only ideas that might work better at different times. Finding your own message is about looking *inward*, not outward. It's about looking inward with honesty.

A great way to start with this is by looking at your lifestyle. For example:

- What do you eat? Are you a bowl of cornflakes type of person or more of a smashed-avocado-on-toast kinda guy?
- What do you wear? Do you leave the house looking like Marilyn Manson, Elton John or Louis Theroux?
- Do you exercise?
- Are you a gamer?
- What films are you into? Do you like anime movies, or do you prefer *The Wolf of Wall Street*?

It may seem silly looking in this much detail, and it's not totally necessary to unpack *every* aspect of your life, but it's imperative to understand what your vibe is so you can better understand what you're portraying to the outside world. Here are three examples of the type of thing you might write:

Message 1

I don't give a fuck what I look like; I just go out in something comfy. I don't give a fuck about being a great guitarist, or anything; I just like cool tunes and guitar bands. I don't give a fuck what people think. I eat bacon butties, and I think life is about having loads of sex with fit people, drinking and having a boss time with your mates.

Message 2

I wouldn't be seen dead in a trench coat; I will only wear fabulous boutique clothing, and I love anything that sparkles. I think life is what you make it, and you gotta go after it and believe in yourself. I absolutely love Mimi Webb, Cardi B and Nicki Minaj. I tried the taster menu at Heston Blumenthal's Fat Duck restaurant last weekend. I was in a long-term relationship, but it all broke apart, and now I'm just pushing on to get over it all.

Message 3

> I'm shy, and I worry what people think of me. I tend to try to avoid being around lots of people. I suffer from bad anxiety and find it difficult to talk to people. I just wear stuff I think is cute, and I'm not too bothered about what I look like. I'm really into The Cranberries and Fleetwood Mac, and I enjoy hanging out with my friends in my house. I'm gay, and I sometimes feel isolated from my family, but my boyfriend has been a rock through all the hard times.

Deciding how to handle these messages is a separate consideration. As I've emphasised in this chapter, the crucial point is that the message resonates genuinely and honestly with your own identity. Later in the book I will guide you through the process of unravelling and refining your message. This narrative lays the foundation for the music you create and the image you project to the world. It can also offer glimpses into your fashion choices, the attitude you convey and the goals you aspire to achieve.

People are extraordinarily diverse and complex. All kinds of interesting stories and oddities can exist in the same individual, and that's exactly what personality is all about. Embrace your flaws and vulnerability as well as your strengths.

Here's a list of ten artists with distinct and different identities and musical messages. You'll immediately have a sense of what each person's message is, from the way they dress, the things they say and the type of music they write:

1. Susan Boyle
2. Elton John
3. Megan Thee Stallion
4. Sam Smith
5. Sam Fender
6. Liam Gallagher
7. George Ezra
8. Ozzy Osbourne
9. Maisie Peters
10. Dua Lipa

When you compare Susan Boyle's 'I Dreamed A Dream' lyrics with, say, those of Megan Thee Stallion's 'Sweetest Pie', it's quite clear that the sentiments of both artists differ wildly. You'll see the same contrast if you take any song from Dua Lipa's catalogue and compare it with Ozzy Osbourne's 'War Pigs'. This distinction is true for any of the artists above, and indeed for any of the artists out there smashing it today. Everyone has a unique identity, and when they wear it, they write about it, they express it authentically, and people take notice and want to be a part of it, no matter what that identity is. Somewhere, somehow, each musician with a clear message finds their tribe.

Look at the following statements, each of which is widely attributed to the artist named in each point. You'll see how these are not mere quotes. Reading the things they say in the press, you get a complete sense of who the people are:

- 'Works of art make rules; rules do not make works of art.' – attributed to Claude Debussy
- 'I don't see myself as an artist; I see myself as just a rock and roll singer who writes an odd tune every now and again.' – attributed to Liam Gallagher
- 'I had trouble distinguishing art from life. I don't now, and I feel much better!' – attributed to Donald Fagen
- 'My approach is just fearless. I'm not afraid to try anything.' – attributed to Stormzy
- 'God will never give you anything you can't handle, so don't stress.' – attributed to Kelly Clarkson
- 'I don't know how to function without music. When I'm not making it, I'm listening to it. It gives me courage and takes care of my mind.' – attributed to Billie Eilish

TRY THIS NOW: The real you

Make notes on the following questions:

- What about you is unique to you?
- What about you is worth talking about?

Remember, it's people that make the music industry go round, not laws, technical skills, memes or fancy inventions. If you can't connect with people on a genuine level, they might ignore you or, at worst, cause you trouble. Let your message shine through authentically. As long as it's true to who you are, your message will captivate those who resonate with it. That's the key to building meaningful connections and making a real impact.

THREE
Make Music

Naturally, the thing a musician must do is make music. There are lots of ways you can go about it, and here are the most important points to keep in mind:

- Have fun
- Keep an eye on why you're doing it
- Develop your taste

If you're interested in becoming a songwriter, this chapter will also show you ideas on how to add finesse to your ideas in a simple way.

What is born talent?

What has talent got to do with anything? Shows like *The X Factor* create an illusion of talent as if it's an ability you possess, like the Force possessed by Jedi. What everyone agrees on is that people who have a talent are those who are naturally good at something without really trying too hard. It's like they have a special ability or skill that comes to them easily. You can see talent in lots of different areas like sports, art, music, writing – pretty much any aspect of human culture. Talent is what makes some people stand out and be recognised. You can work on your talent and get better with practice and hard work, but any talent is typically considered as something you're born with.

I don't believe this for one second. People are *not* born with special talents.

What I see, especially as a mentor, is people of all shapes, sizes and backgrounds have natural interests that were nurtured simply because those people initially showed those interests. That's what talent really is: being super into something and nurturing that passion. The real driving force behind talent is interest, because all the hard work, sweat, late nights and dedication happen only if you genuinely enjoy something. Talent as a mystical or biological predisposition doesn't exist. For example, the reason I got good at the guitar is because I love it, which made me want to get better at playing it. That's it.

Stop fretting about whether you're as good as famous people or those around you. Don't worry about having the X factor. Instead, simply ask yourself: What do I really love doing? If you already know the answer to that question, great! That means you have the makings of being someone who is talented. You simply need to nurture what you love, which is hardly a problem – it's an absolute pleasure!

Seasick Steve is a perfect example of someone who did what he was good at, followed it as far as his love would take him, and then got lots of people to take notice of and be interested in his skills. His skills are limited to a specific area, yes; but they are unique to him and where he wanted to go. For that reason alone he has achieved fame, recognition and a good level of income and standard of lifestyle.

Making yourself good at music

Talents can change and evolve, just as your level of interest in something can change and evolve. No matter what path you choose, there might be areas where you need to improve, but the method you use to make any improvement needs to be authentic.

One way to get some great feedback straight away is to record yourself performing; watching that back will normally make it clear what you need to work on. If that doesn't happen, ask some people you trust for their opinions on your performance. They might be able to give you insight into the way you sing or play, or something about the way you walk, or the way you talk to whatever crowd you have. Either way, a real musician, a real architect or a real student of any art or vocation is glad to know of their mistakes and flaws. Once you recognise yours, you can do something about them. Only delusional idiots think they're perfect in every way, and only delusional idiots don't like to critique themselves.

When you genuinely love something, you don't require a detailed manual on how to express that love. Similarly, it's not a universal rule, for example, that everyone must excel as a technical singer, as that assertion doesn't hold true. If it did, we could easily draft step-by-step instructions for becoming technical singers, and the whole world would be filled with brilliant vocalists.

Success in an industry isn't about mastering every skill; it's about channelling that singular passion for what you love. It's like a fire – while it may require effort to spark the flame with the right kindling, it is the willingness to take action that ultimately brings the flames to life. Once the fire is lit, it naturally attracts others to bask in its warmth.

Success isn't reserved for a select few who luck out. It's all about those who find something they're truly interested in and who weather the difficulties to see where that interest leads. This is why you need to believe in your passion, chase your curiosity, and relish the thrill of exploring your interests.

If you want to make it in the music scene, you gotta create some mind-blowing tracks, and you can only do that by becoming *extremely* good at what you do. Thankfully, that's no trouble at all for someone who's *extremely interested*!

A sliding scale

In the music industry today there are successful people at all levels. Some people may not understand basic music concepts at all, while others can play highly complicated pieces with note-for-note perfection. This bears no relevance at all to the success side of things, except for the fact that your musical skills must match up to what you're intending to become. Many of today's biggest stars didn't go to music school, and they don't read or write music. There's absolutely no correlation between education and success in the industry – with or without formal education, you can be successful.

Let's think about why you should bother improving your musical skills. There are two main reasons:

1. The better you are at music, the more likely you'll be to create great music when you write, record or perform.

2. The more you know about music, the more you'll appreciate and understand the different kinds of music out there, which will only feed into and help you on the previous point.

As an experienced musician, I've learned that knowing a lot about music lets me notice, enjoy and detect small details that others miss, which can only ever help me write, record and perform. Conversely, people like my brother Josh, who doesn't know much about music, can still enjoy popular and fun tunes without thinking about those details. Getting better music skills doesn't (necessarily) mean studying Beethoven, but it does mean at the very least exploring all that music has to offer, and in the process discovering what you're best at and what you're really into.

For those who want to get better at music to succeed, there are two things you can do:

1. Improve your technical skills

2. Figure out what kind of music you like most

It's important to know that a guitarist like Noel Gallagher might not be able to play a song by Django Reinhardt, and he might not even want to. To most people, though, Noel Gallagher might seem like a better guitarist than Django Reinhardt. That's because what is 'better' to most people is not down to technique – it's down to *taste*.

TRY THIS NOW: Broadening your music mindset

Go to a streaming platform and look at the playlists you listen to. I dare you to delete them all, or at least to set up an entirely different account, so you don't fall into the usual trap of listening to the same stuff.

Once you've done that, create an empty playlist and only add things to it that are new to you.

After that, go exploring! Have a look at the '50s, '60s, '70s... right the way through to present day. Also, if you like a particular song, download the album, not only the song. Also, don't look only at different eras – explore diverse countries and genres. You'd be amazed at what you find when you look for French music, German music, Japanese music, and so on. You can also search by instrument, for example solo drum music, acoustic guitar music, etc.

This all helps you to discover new music and ideas and to develop your taste. Don't forget to share this with friends, and try to learn or dance to some tracks. Have fun!

Good taste becomes hugely important a little later on in your career.

Write down some new genres or themes you'd like to look into.

What matters most

What makes music good isn't how clever and complicated it is. It's nothing to do with fitting in lots of musical tricks or complex things. Instead, it's about doing what the music requires and expressing what sounds good. For music students still at college, this can be really hard to understand. Colleges focus primarily on making you technically skilled. You have to learn scales, pass exams, read music, and so on. In truth, though, none of those skills guarantee any success in the music industry. There are plenty of Grade 8 guitarists who can't get a gig in a pub!

The reason for this is because delving deeply into the study of music typically demands:

- An extensive amount of time
- A considerable dose of humility
- An immeasurable volume of repetition and concentration

Often, people with such a laser-like focus on their skills alone are either too shy or too hugely egotistical about their skills to promote themselves. They may lose sight of the vast world around them, one that consistently and with great demand rewards and pays those who offer entertaining service, are personable, enjoy themselves and recognise that captivating a crowd of beer-drinking people doesn't necessarily require mind-blowing technique and profound theory. Sometimes all you need are four chords, the volume as loud as possible, and the ability to discuss a price!

Most important is to focus on honing your skills in the area that interests you the most. If you want to be a DJ, why waste time studying classical composers like Beethoven? If you dream of being a pop star, why would you need to spend time learning to read sheet music? If jazz guitar is your passion, instead of worrying about putting on an entertaining show, concentrate on improving your guitar skills. If you want to be a songwriter, don't worry about soloing at the same pace as Miles Davis – focus instead on singers, lyrics, poetry or humour. This is all about looking at exactly what is intrinsic to your direction.

Honing your skills is all about striking a balance between what you need to know and what interests you artistically. Some things in music will simply sound cool to you, and you might not know exactly why… and that's OK.

The second thing to bear in mind is that the more you know and understand, the deeper your appreciation and awareness of music becomes. Increased knowledge opens up more possibilities and directions. For example, if you only know songs by Lewis Capaldi, you won't ever be able to comprehend, create anything similar to or tackle performing something by

Jacob Collier or Snarky Puppy. Digging deeper into your musical skills will only improve your ability to connect the dots between all musical areas. Having a range of skills makes it that much easier to switch between music styles and call on them whenever you're writing or performing, or when you're simply listening to and enjoying music.

Many successful musicians follow their gut feeling, and they concentrate on what sounds great rather than overthinking everything. Simply pick up the instrument and see what happens. Don't be afraid to get it wrong.

Creating a good workflow

Our brains are constantly reminding us that there are better things we could be doing with our time. I've learned that careful time management is crucial to allow you to practise well and to commit fully to any mental tasks.

It's essential to create good workflows in a purpose-built space. If you're interested in becoming a better songwriter, for example, make sure your home studio is already set up, good to go and ready for you to record. Make the experience *only* about the task – only about the music – not about troubleshooting and pointless admin.

Before you even start, make sure you are on top of anything that might distract you or slow down your workflow, including:

- Upgrade old and slow computers.
- Invest in decent kit and maintain electrical equipment.
- Replace any damaged cables.
- Restring any instruments that need it.
- Clear away trash, tidy up and vacuum your office or rehearsal room.
- Make shelving units, colour-code files and put up attractive artwork.
- Stay up to date with bills or rentals, leases or mortgages.
- Keep a working kettle and good coffee on hand, and always have food in the fridge.

With all this in place, you won't be troubleshooting equipment and lack of desk space every time you want to get down to work. Crafting a pleasant atmosphere in your workspace, together with finding the right people to be with, will empower your process.

Dan Dare: Be proactive, not reactive

Few people have earned their credentials and proven their work ethic and creative prowess like Dan Dare. Born and raised in Southall, London, Dan first made waves in the grime scene as an MC with The Gritty Committee, collaborating with acts like True Tiger and Dynasty Crew on the pirate radio station Freeze FM. His early passion for beat making soon led him to music production, where he secured major collaborations with Giggs and Juelz Santana on 'Bright Lights', working alongside ZDOT and Richard Kylea Cowie Jr, better known as Wiley.

Dan credits much of his growth as a songwriter to the time he spent with his close friends Ryan Keen and Toby Faulkner. They were living in a bedsit in Hackney, sharing everything, all aspiring songwriters trying to do the best they could with what they had. They had terrible but loud speakers, and they made beats all day. They wrote songs, invited people over and had a great time.

It was only when they signed publishing deals and started releasing music that people tried to sway their identities and influence what they did. At the time, Dan said, Ryan was on a world tour with Ed Sheeran, playing incredible gigs. Toby was writing songs with his brother and having loads of success. Meanwhile, Dan was still working on beat stuff, watching the success happen around him, thinking, *Maybe I need to do a bit more of that.*

Dan says he started taking inspiration from everyone, including learning a lot from Ryan and Toby about melody and songwriting. Dan stuck with honing his art, and his career took a significant leap when he teamed up with Nick Worthington, founder of 679 Recordings, who introduced him to groundbreaking artists like Rudimental and MNEK. While sharing a studio at Major Toms for three years, he co-wrote and co-produced Syron's debut singles 'Here' and 'Breaking', under Black Butter Records.

After forming the songwriting duo Kolidescopes with John Courtidis, Dan played a key role in co-writing and co-producing the global hit 'Head & Heart' by Joel Corry and MNEK. The track was number one for a staggering six weeks in the UK and ten weeks in Ireland, and it now has over 1.2 billion streams.

When asked what advice he would give to aspiring artists, Dan said that the internet nowadays is a game changer; that you can message Beyoncé on Instagram, and she might actually see it. While Dan was growing up, artists were idolised because they felt out of reach.

He said his advice is to research online. Find out who the managers and publishers are. Be proactive, not reactive. Go to open mic nights, as you never know who you'll meet. You might see a terrible singer on stage, but their guitarist could be incredible, and that's how bands come together.

> Dan also explained that collaboration is key – you need to meet like-minded people, so it's important to go to open mic nights, send emails, reach out to people. 'You never know what could come from it,' he says.
>
> Dan's career continues to thrive and has earned him a BMI Award and nominations for both an Ivor Novello Award and a BRIT Award. His extensive list of songwriting collaborations includes Noah Kahan, Charli XCX, Dillon Francis, Becky Hill, Fodera, Hussain Manawer, Chris Malinchak, Liam Payne, Selah Sue, WSTRN, Mario, Sam Feldt, REI AMI, Marina and the Diamonds, and A7S. For more info, visit https://dandare.carrd.co.
>
> You can hear the interview on my *More in the Moni* podcast at www.moreinthemoni.com.

I've learned that being a great musician isn't just about having lots of theoretical knowledge. It's about *doing something* with what you know.

In my own personal practice (for those who want to know), I have one main area of focus: the new stuff that I'll perform soon on tours or sessions – the stuff that pays the bills – the rest is supplementary. I do the work I'm paid to do, and I don't lift a finger unless it's for one of my clients or associates. Sometimes I need to learn material, which sometimes might be how to use a computer program. Other times I might have to build a shelving unit or wire a pedal board. In any case, the key is making it fun and getting organised and in a workflow. I always try to make theoretical sessions fun, organic and practical, and I tend to avoid arduous sessions delivered by teachers on YouTube and rambling through inert facts. I mainly concentrate on the discovery of new sounds and new ideas, and how those make me feel and how I can replicate them or apply them.

A great tip if you have any memory exercise to achieve (like learning a song, memorising lines, etc) is to never do it all in one room. Make sure you work on it while you're on the bus, at the beach, in a bar. Include different sights, sounds, smells and textures wherever possible, and the stuff will stick. Play the song on a new guitar, do it really loudly, do it quietly, walk around, stand up, go outside, put lights on or turn them all off. No matter what you learn – even if it isn't music – this will totally solidify whatever you're practising and cut out loads of wasted energy.

There are many ways that one can improve technically. It's vital that those improvements serve your core purpose and that they contribute to the meaning of your message if you're going to be able to internalise them to use them in growing your career.

FOUR
Explore Your Craft

Part of the route to being a successful songwriting artist is learning how to write great music and how best to record it. Songwriters get inspired by their own experiences and emotions, and what they observe in the world helps bring their songs to life. In short, they tap into their message.

What is the song for?

Before you even begin songwriting, you should save yourself a load of heartache and hassle by asking yourself straight away: *What am I writing these songs for?* This is the first and most important question, because if the song is for you and you want to express your innermost passions, turmoil and darkest desires, you need not read any further on how to write a song. Just write it. Let loose, make it as long or as short as you want, say what you want, use any instrument you like, and record it wherever and however you want to. There's nothing anybody could say to you that would ever be of any use in telling you how to express yourself.

However, things are different if you're looking to be a songwriter because you want your songs to be recognised, signed and on the radio, or you want them so you can pass a course or achieve some kind of criteria. Then you need to know the things that the industry wants, or what a course or a radio station wants, and to start adapting your approach.

You have to understand that if you think what you're doing is cool, that's great, but it doesn't necessarily mean that anybody else will think it's cool or that they will give you any money for it. This is where – and *only* where – songwriting tips, tricks, pointers and advice suddenly become relevant.

I met a songwriter who refused to compromise in any way. He was desperate to get his music on BBC Introducing, but every time he submitted a track to the uploader, he got rejected. Feeling totally despondent after about six tries, he asked for my help. When I looked at his material, my first impression was that the quality of the recording wasn't great, which radio doesn't like. More to the point, though, each of his songs were seven to eleven minutes long! No radio station normally has enough airtime to devote to an eight-minute track, even if it's from Prince's unreleased tapes! Despite me saying something like, 'You know if you just made the song shorter and took some of the guitars off, you could probably get it on the radio?', this artist was totally blinkered. He thought what he was doing was right, and he consequently never got it on air.

This is an example of not understanding or researching what the music is *for*. This songwriter thought what he'd written was for getting signed and for playing on the radio, but it wasn't. It was for him, because he loved it. He should have recognised that what he'd created was in fact a labour of love, not a flagship radio track for a new artist. He should've simply recorded it, released it on Spotify, listened to it in his bedroom, or put it on a download or a CD for people to enjoy.

Ask yourself whether you're in this to get somewhere, or if you're in it purely for the love of writing. Either way is great, but you need to be clear on this. There's no one right way to write a song – it's all about your personal message and what the song is for. For example, if you want to be a pop writer like Dua Lipa, Olivia Rodrigo or Sam Smith, that's great. However, if your song is hitting your personal message but doesn't have a huge chorus or have the right production, then it quite simply won't go anywhere.

This is all about what you're writing for. When you're clear about where you want your music to go, it will inform your decisions on how to write it, and later, how to produce it and market it too.

Smashing things together to create something new

Understanding things like melodies, structures, harmonies and all that technical stuff is relevant, but instead of diving into manuals on *how* to be a better songwriter, it's more important to ask yourself *what* you think makes songs great.

Here are some questions that will start you heading in the right direction:

- What do you really love about the music you listen to?

- What are the similarities between the artists you love – do they sound the same? Do they look the same?

- What are the factors that make them sound the way they do? Eg are they electronic, or do they feature more organic elements?

- Are there any of those elements you could potentially incorporate into your own tunes?

EXPLORE YOUR CRAFT

Some of the greatest songwriters of the last five decades are not shy at all about saying they listened to or were inspired by one tune then smashed it with another one, and that's how they created their own thing. Here are just a few examples:

- Carlos Santana smashed Blues with Latin music.
- Kanye West sampled Ray Charles's 'I Got a Woman' (a big band genre) and smashed it with modern day hip hop.
- The Police smashed reggae music with '80s pop.
- The 1975 have smashed '80s pop with Indie and Art House.
- Oasis smashed The Beatles with Les Paul guitars.
- Sabrina Carpenter smashed '80s pop with retro vintage '70s synths.
- Ed Sheeran took singer-songwriter acoustic music and smashed it together with pop production and rap/hip-hop influences.
- Sam Fender took '90s indie music and mixed it with '80s structures.
- Jacob Collier smashes nearly everything together, including the kitchen sink, and the results are boundlessly beautiful.

It doesn't matter which elements you play with – when you take two things you love and mix them together some way, you always end up with something new. It might not work every time, but it's a great way to create something fresh and exciting with nearly no thought at all.

It pays in the modern music business to be mixing things that are current with things that are retro. Familiarity is what makes people take note of your music. When they think *Ah – that sounds a bit like…*, the chances are much higher that they'll latch onto your music. Algorithms are then much more likely to playlist you in similar genres you're aiming for, and brands are more likely to position you on the same lineup, etc.

> **Andy Dunlop: Passion and fandom**
>
> Andy absolutely loved music from the start. He was all about following his passion, and he didn't care much for school. Music was like magic to him, and he couldn't get enough of it. He felt like music could take him anywhere and make him feel all sorts of emotions.
>
> Andy discovered early on that he was talented at playing the guitar. He could make beautiful sounds come out of it, and he felt like he was creating a whole world. He realised that music had this special power to make people feel things and bring them closer together. He even recorded interesting sounds he heard around him, like the noise of a

café's air conditioning fan or the melody of church bells, and used these recordings in his songs.

As Andy grew up, his love for music grew too. He was super-passionate about writing songs and playing music. He got together with some friends who loved music as much as he did, and they started a band. The band was called Travis, and Andy was their guitarist.

In 2003 Travis released an album called *The Man Who*. It became a huge hit, selling millions of copies in the UK. This success didn't happen out of nowhere. It was because of Andy's talent (with the support of his band), his hard work and his strong belief in the music he was making.

I was curious about how Andy managed to achieve such success with Travis, so I asked him if he attributed that to anything from his past. He said that he only listened to classical music when he was very young, but when he was around eleven or twelve, that fed into proper rock music like AC/DC.

He grinned as he recalled his first gig at the age of twelve, watching Status Quo perform, which he said was great because it was so loud and wild. His friend's dad had taken Andy and his friend, both rocking denim jackets covered in patches. It was a seated concert, and the dad said he'd wait for them at the top, where he could keep an eye on them. Then some bikers at the front lifted the boys onto their shoulders, and they spent the entire gig up there, waving at Status Quo. 'It was so loud,' said Andy, 'but I was like "This is what I like now!"'

That little taste of music's power and of the joy it brought Andy was enough to light a fire in him, setting him on a path that ultimately led to his success. He said at first it was all about rock music – Queen, Status Quo, Black Sabbath, AC/DC – which all had a huge impact on him. Then he met Fran Healy, who introduced Andy to a bunch of different genres, and their styles blended perfectly. After they started gigging and eventually touring, it all became kind of a blur, he said.

After all the fame, chance encounters, hard work and endless dedication, Andy found himself back in the education scene. He started teaching students how to make it in the music world. He says he thinks it all comes down to taste – you can be an amazing musician, but if your taste in music is garbage, it won't get you anywhere.

I asked him if taste could be taught, and Andy said that while you can't force someone to have good taste, you can inspire them with truly awesome stuff.

It blew my mind that Andy could recall these significant moments in his career, even though he didn't have some big master plan. He simply did what he loved, refined his taste and let the world come to him. Success found him because he rocked at something he adored, not because he was only after money, fame, or a nine-times platinum album.

You can hear the whole interview on my *More in the Moni* podcast at www.moreinthemoni.com.

Keeping this simple

A song doesn't have to be clever. It just has to sound cool. You don't have to be Shakespeare with your lyrics, and you don't have to be Miles Davis with your melodies. The song only has to hit the mark you're aiming at. If your goal is to be an indie band selling out London's Brixton Academy, then you need to be writing tunes that connect with that audience. You don't have to know all the techniques and clever chords in the handbook. Rather than following a strict formula, you need to embrace your own musical message and let it guide you.

If we take one of the messages from Chapter Two as a starting point, you can see how that message might provide some of the grounds for the sonics and the sound of it all. Looking at message number one, you may be able to see straight away that it bears some useful indications as to what you should be aiming for, what lyrics you ought to be writing, which influences you need to pay attention to, and the types of chords and structures you need to understand. Let's go through it line by line.

Message 1

> I don't give a fuck what I look like; I just go out in something comfy. I don't give a fuck about being a great guitarist, or anything; I just like cool tunes and guitar bands. I don't give a fuck

what people think. I eat bacon butties, and I think life is about having loads of sex with fit people, drinking and having a boss time with your mates.

The first sentence says 'I don't give a fuck'. To me that is an indication that the chords should be simple, with no fucks given. The lyrics need to be obnoxious, and the music and the way it's recorded can be stripped back, honest, open and with no frills. Immediately, you can discard anything that is too sentimental or too complicated or has too difficult a meaning to penetrate. It should be simple, on the nose and straight to the point.

'I just go out in something comfy.' There's your stage clothes. Don't wear anything fancy.

'I just like cool tunes and guitar bands.' This is about what inspires you. Consider Inhaler, Grace Bowers, Oasis, Wet Leg, Declan McKenna, Olivia Rodrigo, Royston Club, Jamie T, Oscar Lang, The Strokes, etc, as your influences. Don't ever include any synths in your music that are too '80s or anthemic, unless it's enhancing the guitar. Also, your song length probably should therefore be around three minutes; and the types of chords you use should be no more than about three or four chords, with a quicker tempo. Eventually, you'd likely be aiming to pitch your music for Radio 1 or Radio 2 in the UK; or KEXP-FM 90.3, WIOW 102.3 DB – WOW! Radio, or SomaFM – Indie Pop Rocks!, WVRK, KMRQ in the US.

'I eat bacon butties and I think life is about having loads of sex with fit people, drinking and having a boss time with your mates.' This is what your lyrics are about and, ultimately, what your social media will reflect too. Go out and party hard, take lots of photos and videos, and get into all kinds of hilarious situations. Write a song the minute you get in the next day, or at least the minute after you've eaten your bacon butty. Then upload the pictures, the lifestyle and a short taster of some of your songs to your socials. Keep talking in songs and in socials about nightlife, mad parties, and about life in the suburbs and the streets and the bars. Keep it consistent – remember, you're playing the long game.

If at some point you were to think, *I also actually enjoy quiet walks in the park, and I love listening to Aretha Franklin when I'm chilling out*, then simply add that to your message. You could write some more introspective tunes about this, which will also show to both your fans and friends that you're not a total maniac and you have a deeper side!

None of this has to be clever. It just has to be honest and hitting the brief, as in the example above. Anyone watching that artist, listening to the music and looking at the socials feed, will feel that everything is cohesive, together and authentic. The trick is not to come across as confused in any way.

You simply have to find interesting ways of saying things. It doesn't even have to mean much at all if you don't want it to, as long as that really is your message. 'I Am the Walrus' by The Beatles doesn't necessarily have to mean anything. Michael Jackson famously said 'I am a vegetable' in 'Wanna Be Startin' Somethin'', purely because it sounded rhythmic and was great to sing. David Bowie, in 'We Are the Dead', could have said 'I wanna have sex with you', but instead he said 'I love you in your fuck-me pumps'.

The same can be said of the chords you use – you don't need to overthink them at all. The song 'Dreams' by Fleetwood Mac is literally two chords the whole way through, apart from a very short bridge section, which briefly takes it away from the pattern. Lola Young's 'Messy' follows this identical pattern of two chords providing all the harmonic material right the way through. Ed Sheeran freely admits to using the same chord progression over and over again in various combinations, but it still works and he continues to be extremely creative with his lyric writing.

The recording and production process

What most people want is a recording deal. Actually getting into a studio can be really costly, depending on what your aims and objectives are, so it's good to consider what the process is for before spending a huge budget.

The process of recording can be categorised in two ways:

1. Doing it yourself
2. Utilising a professional studio

The determining factors are time and budget.

Throughout your entire journey, you want to be minimising expenses and maximising your impact, and the good news is that it's possible. For most artists and labels, I recommend as an artist you should have, at the very least, a laptop and some basic recording software to grasp the essence of the process. I suggest considering software such as GarageBand, Logic Pro X, Ableton, Pro Tools and Cubase. Excellent online resources like BandLab (which is *free*) are also available. Furthermore, there are numerous production courses, YouTube videos, internships, online tutorials and similar materials that explain how to use these tools in straightforward terms.

Developing the ability to create decent demos is crucial. In the fast-paced economy of TikTok, viral videos and charts like New Music Friday (which run for only one week), generating content quickly is key. If you've only got five songs to your name, that won't make much of an impact. If you have twenty-five song snippets and twenty-five videos (cut in half for TikTok, so really fifty videos' worth), then you have a much more convincing platform for people to look at. Imagine looking at an Instagram page with only five pictures. You'd immediately conclude that this person doesn't do much, and that's exactly what labels and fans do. You *need* to generate the content, so at the basic level you want to be making stuff to a generally good standard, without it costing you money to record it each time.

This standard is generally the norm. There isn't a single decent breakthrough artist that doesn't have high-quality audio or video. The demand for writing so much music, however, is a positive. Not only does it aid you in your songwriting development; it also accelerates your understanding of the more intricate production procedures.

If you have some money and want to record your music properly, then again ask yourself, *Why?* Why should you spend money on a recording rather than doing it yourself? Well, the reason could be that somebody with some industry clout is willing to pay for or back those recordings in some way or has a platform to catapult them once they're done. If you have spare cash and fancy paying for things out of your pocket, then that's great – your stuff will sound amazing, which goes a long way to convincing people that you're serious.

If you don't already have funds for this, you shouldn't feel the need to flog all of your wages on a Neumann

U87 Ai Studio Set and studio-quality demos. Instead, focus on delivering emotive and passionate performances during the recording process to effectively convey the intended message of your music. Capture expressive nuances and dynamics to add life and depth to your tracks.

If you feel that collaborating with a skilled audio engineer or producer will enhance your chances and you can afford it, then go for it. If you don't, this isn't necessarily a setback. Often this type of thing can be explored or greater expressed in co-writes with other musicians because they can share the costs of an audio engineer or producer. The goal is not just to create great music, but to create great *sounding* music. However you do that, whether with or without the help of audio technicians, is entirely dependent on your own skills as an engineer.

Years ago I created a programme for musicians (later developed for a much broader definition of artists) to help them with exactly this problem – cost vs time vs direction. The programme seeks to help artists with funding options, cost mitigations, mentoring and a whole host of resources such as studio time and management to help reach their goals. I hold regular meetings with its members to make sure they understand their own roles to play, as well as discussing strategy, collaboration and ideas for pitching.

TRY THIS NOW: Having a realistic purpose

Is the purpose of your recordings to sell something and make money? If so, you want to make it for less than you sell it. For example, if it costs you £1k to create an album and you stand to earn £5k, then it's a worthwhile investment.

Most serious albums will, depending on the artist, cost anything from £10k to £100k to produce, so you need to think of the purpose.

Is it to get you recognition from a label? If so, what label?

Do you know someone in the label to get it to, or is it a shot in the dark? If it's a shot in the dark, why (potentially) waste the money? Aren't you better off spending that cash making something decent to give to your fans so you can build your audience, meaning you can approach a label with some solid numbers at a later date?

There's no right or wrong answer here, but it pays to think about *Why*? What is the purpose of your recordings?

The importance of co-writes

Co-writing offers more than just the fun of collaboration. It opens doors and expands your creative reach. Working with other musicians and artists can also enrich your music, exposing you to new ideas and opportunities.

If you have a clear vision for your song and know its purpose, there are two main options of how to engage others in helping you bring it to life, especially in recording or production:

1. Pay those people to execute your vision.

2. Co-write with them, giving them a creative stake and a share in potential success if the song gets picked up by a label or gains traction on platforms like TikTok.

If you choose not to co-write, you retain full ownership of your masters, but for most this isn't financially feasible. Collaborators also bring fresh perspectives, spotting things you might miss and sometimes even guiding your music in exciting new directions.

The second option is common in many industries. Could you partner with someone, allowing them a share of the profits in exchange for their resources? This lets you start albums or EPs without needing all the upfront capital. It's similar to the *Dragon's Den* model: participants bring an idea they can't fund alone, so they seek the Dragons' support in return for a stake in their business. Studio producers, casting directors, chefs and other professionals often work this way. By teaming up, you share both the risk and the reward.

When it comes to recording, it's wise to spend strategically, knowing exactly what you're paying for rather than simply aiming for 'high-quality recordings'. Understanding the distinct roles of both producers and engineers is essential if you're working within a budget. This way, every dollar helps you get closer to realising your creative vision.

Cam Blackwood: Recording every major label solo artist because of George Ezra

Cam loved music deeply and was famous for creating wonderful melodies. He had the chance to work in renowned recording studios all over London, impressing everyone with his brilliant music.

In 2010 he started his own studio, called Voltaire Road Studios, in the vibrant neighbourhood of Clapham. With the help of Echo Beach Management, Cam's reputation skyrocketed as he collaborated with well-known artists such as George Ezra and London Grammar. He also worked with soulful singers like Billie Marten and the mesmerising voice of Jack Savoretti. Many artists wanted his creative touch, including British Sea Power, Alabama 3, Florence and the Machine, CSS and We Are Scientists. Cam Blackwood's musical adventure continued, leaving a legacy of beautiful melodies and inspiring artists.

I caught up with Cam and asked him about honing writing skills and the importance of working with people. He told me he'd always thought he'd love to be a successful producer but never really knew what that meant. He originally thought he could be this guy who could turn up two hours late for a session, or just go out partying, but he very quickly realised that wasn't the case. He also spent a long time trying to work out what music to work on and what music not to work on.

Cam says that when you start to get traction with the music you're making, it's very tempting to say yes to everything. It's flattering that the head of Polydor will come and say hi; or the head of Island will send you an email, saying 'We've got this new artist we want you to work with.' Cam said yes to a lot of things he shouldn't have and admitted that he's probably got a lot more misses than hits. Cam says his management saved him from many misses, but they didn't see his success growing so quickly – George Ezra was huge in the UK, and 'Budapest' was massive worldwide.

Cam says he gets asked at some point to work with every singer-songwriter signed in the UK to a major label, including Gavin James, Tom Walker, George Ezra, Jack Savoretti and James TW. Ed Sheeran is probably the only one he hasn't been involved with, all because of George Ezra!

You can and should hear the full interview on my *More in the Moni* podcast at www.moreinthemoni.com.

Getting the word out

Once you've recorded your songs, seek feedback from trusted friends, musicians or mentors to help refine your work. This approach applies to any creative project: if you've made something great, tell people about it, and see what they think. Constructive criticism can be invaluable for fine-tuning your music. Remember, though, everyone has an opinion, so you need to focus on two key things:

1. What resonates with your fans
2. What could appeal to potential investors or labels

If you have a strong fan base, your music might be easier for management or a label to pitch. If you have quality songs with few followers, though, it's important to listen to what those who can help you pitch may suggest. If you have access to a well-connected manager or lawyer, they can likely pitch bold ideas. Otherwise, if a deal is your goal, you may need to adjust your music or strategy to align with current trends.

A&R reps often give feedback like, *It's great, but the chorus should be bigger*, or *Nice, but the production could be different*. These comments often reflect what they think they can sell. Be cautious if someone praises everything without critique – they might have high connections, but that could also lead to you having unrealistic expectations for your project.

Know who your music is for and where you're aiming to go. When your songs are ready, share them on streaming platforms and social media to reach a wider audience. Promote through live shows, videos, interviews and collaborations. You never know who might be watching!

Creating something great is a journey, so stay open to feedback and keep evolving. Use live performances – even smaller gigs or open mics – to test your songs with real audiences. This experience can reveal what resonates live and help you refine the arrangement, tempo or structure as you grow as an artist.

FIVE
Perform Live

Something absurd in the world is happening right now. AI can now do everything! Well, not *everything*, but it's taking people's jobs left, right and centre and doing them without sleep, without being paid and without safeguarding or any human issues whatsoever. This is an amazing time in human history because it forces us to evaluate what we're *really* good at without being simply 'worker drones'. The simple fact is that machines can better us in nearly every capacity, and they're only going to get better (or worse, depending on your point of view).

When it comes to the looming threat to the music business, for example, you can ask a robot from anywhere in the world – while you're on the toilet, on a plane, in a café, on a train journey, etc – to make a tune for you. It'll make it in half the time that a musician could and with none of the expense, none of the ego and zero faff with licensing or intellectual property arguments.

It could be that within less than two years, robots will do lots of things, including creating records that sound as polished as a Beyoncé track in under twenty seconds. Until that time comes, making recordings and using recording methods are vital. Even DJs and backing tracks will be replaced, or at least enhanced almost 90%, by computers one day. It wouldn't surprise me to see Chat GPT doing a set at Glastonbury.

The rise of computer technology has improved synthesisers, made recording ubiquitous and accessible for everyone (you can record great demos on your phone now) and made all that tedious mic positioning all but redundant. If computers can sing, play music and make recordings better than people, what's most important for fans and artists alike is performing *live*. The moments where people gather together and have fun is the one thing that will not change, ever.

Delivering a great live performance can be done in a local bar as well as at the gigantic festivals. It's about being aware of your audience no matter who they are and connecting with them.

Tommy Emmanuel: The guitar virtuoso who plays from the heart

Born on 31 May 1955, in the heart of Australia, William Thomas Emmanuel – known as Tommy – was destined to leave an indelible mark on the music scene. From an early age, he was captivated by the sounds of the guitar, and it wasn't long before his incredible skill and his approach to music and life set him apart from everyone else.

His solo work has earned him countless awards, and his influence on the acoustic guitar world is undeniable. In 2010 he was appointed a Member of the Order of Australia (AM). The following year he was inducted into the Australian Roll of Renown. By 2019, MusicRadar had named him as one of the top ten acoustic guitarists in the world.

Beyond the accolades and the awards, it's Tommy's down-to-earth personality and his authenticity that truly make him special. The way he plays is not only about technique – it's about the pure, unfiltered joy that radiates from every note. Whether on stage or in the studio, his music is a reflection of his genuine passion. Audiences can feel it instantly; the joy he feels in his playing is contagious. It's as if, in every performance (and there are a lot of them!), he's offering you a piece of his heart. As one fan put it, 'When Tommy plays, you don't just hear the music – you feel it.'

Tommy puts it simply: 'When I was a kid, I wanted to be in showbusiness. Now I just want to be in the happiness business. I make music, and you get happy.'[1]

Tommy's commitment to spreading happiness through music has shaped his career, as he's become known for his ability to bring an infectious joy with every gig. It's almost impossible to leave a Tommy Emmanuel show without a smile on your face, because his happiness is as joyous as his music.

In a world where trends often eclipse artistry, Tommy's unwavering authenticity has become his trademark. His music is a reminder that in an age of noise and distractions, there is still room for genuine expression.

With four Country Music Awards of Australia, two Australian Entertainment Mo Awards, multiple Grammy nominations, ARIA Awards, and a shelf full of Best Acoustic Guitarist titles, Tommy's place in the music world is firmly established. His tours have sold out globally, and he continues to inspire guitarists and music lovers everywhere.

I had the chance to catch up with Tommy mid-tour to discuss his thoughts on performing live and building a lasting audience. He explained that, regardless of social media, you still have to build and create. He said that it's up to you – make some good songs, and make sure that what you do is rock solid. You need your arrangements to be strong and your song choices to be good, and your performance needs to be 100%. Tommy maintains that others can see if you're giving them everything, and that will help you build an audience. People are not stupid, he says – they can tell if you're full of shit or not – so it's all about the quality and integrity of what you do. 'That's the bottom line, because that will shine through like a light.'

Tommy's words are a powerful reminder of the importance of authenticity, both in music and in life.

You can hear the full, exclusive interview on my *More in the Moni* podcast at www.moreinthemoni.com.

Putting on a show

Everyone needs to perform live. It is the acid test of a good musician, no matter if you're a DJ or a songwriter. It's also an opportunity to have lots of fun and dramatically increase your impact. When Wet Leg performed on the Park Stage at Glastonbury in 2022, it instantly catapulted them into the limelight because they became known for their charisma, deadpan delivery and participation with the audience. Arguably, their music was in full circulation before that moment, but it was the live scene that really got everyone's attention. People are what make your music get noticed, and coincidentally, people are also what pays your bills.

It takes a lot to put on a show. Not many people truly understand the effort involved in performing a gig in the pub, let alone what it takes to put on a set at the halftime Super Bowl. Shows can be categorised into two types:

1. **Cover gigs:** where you cover somebody else's material
2. **Original gigs:** where you play your own original songs

Cover gigs

Cover gigs are always in demand from the hospitality industry. They range from high-stakes, quality corporate shows right down to gigs at Irish bars, restaurants, garden parties, and so on. You name it – if there's a space where people have fun, you can do a gig there.

With open mic gigs, all you need to do is find one and turn up, put your name down and do a good job. These are great for testing material.

Otherwise, getting the gig all comes down to one thing: hustling. If you're touting for work in bars, in clubs, at weddings, on cruise ships, and so on, you have to be able to go and sell yourself to local promoters and bar owners, or whoever else is in charge, and convince them that you're good enough for them to pay you.

This is harder than you think, so naturally the more resources you have to demonstrate your skills, the easier it will be for you to get the work. You might want to invest in high-quality video and photographs, a website, and a strong biography with some decent track record. The greater content you have on all fronts, the more work you're likely to get. Over time you'll get better at discussing your fees, creating better shows, learning more material and maybe even getting agents to book you into the higher-paying work. You simply have to get on with all this – buy the gear you need, and get out there hustling.

Original gigs

Putting on your own show works in a completely different way. First you need to understand that nobody in their right mind will pay you to play your own music. It generates no money for bar owners, and the punters don't know your songs (yet!).

Typically, to support the music scene, most venues either host a night featuring multiple artists (eg 'Battle of the Bands') or cover their costs by selling you the space. That way, regardless if it's a sellout or there are only a few stragglers, the venue or promoter knows they're covered financially.

If you're wanting to become a signed artist, you *need* to be gigging in the bars and clubs, you need to be making money, and you need to be getting more fans to your originals shows. A combination of learning covers, writing originals and putting them on strategically will achieve this. Here's a step-by-step guide:

1. Learn some covers and fill your diary with gigs. You need to pay the rent and cover your costs. Cover gigs also help you hone your craft. While you're on your cover shows, you can be plugging your material by weaving the odd song into your set. If you do this, the ratio should be about 90% covers to 10% originals.

2. Rent a venue space or agree on a split with the owner, for example on costs vs tickets sold (not too big, something like a fifty-person capacity or less) and set a date far off in the future, preferably about three or four months away.

3. Sell, sell, sell your tickets. Good ticket sales will cover the cost of the venue and prove to the venue that you can sell shows. Don't, under any circumstances, let anyone in for free. Don't drop your ticket price under £5 because that looks desperate. You have three or four months to sell thirty to fifty tickets. If you can't do that, there's something wrong!

4. Reap the rewards of playing a sold-out show, plastering all over your socials how busy it was.

Next you can do a deal with the venue to do exactly the same thing again in another three to four months' time. You are now also in a position to secure some deals with the venue, because you've proven yourself. For example, could you get the venue hire a bit cheaper? Could you get some money off the doormen or the promo?

Later on, the delicate balance between cover gigs and original gigs becomes vital for brokering deals for you, so get into the habit early. Most people waste all their money doing tours of thirty dates all over the country, playing to no one, and they wonder why labels and managers aren't interested. Focus your strategy, hone your message and make your live shows meaningful.

Improvising and hustling

Putting on these shows requires good hustling skills, and hustling is always about being able to improvise – in life and on the stage.

Improvising is all about creativity. It's about *Let's see what happens* rather than *Here's something I made earlier*. If you think about it, when you're talking to a friend, you improvise your words – you don't rehearse what you're going to say. Some people may have a broader vocabulary than you or have more knowledge in a specific field, but they're still making what they say up on the spot, if with a bit more structure around it. Improvisation is all about the willingness to explore and put yourself out there.

When you're getting great at performing live, you should know that making mistakes is normal. Riding these blunders out is a big factor in overcoming nerves, and I highly recommend the skill of learning to improvise on the spot. Mistakes will always happen, not only while you're playing music, but also due to how the show is set up and run. Problems might come up with the lights, with the sound or even with members of the audience. Just about anything can go wrong and mess up a performance. That's when the ability to improvise becomes crucial.

There are musicians who have made entire careers out of improvisation. The most notable of course are in the blues and jazz genres, for example Muddy Waters, Robert Johnson, Miles Davis and Dave Brubeck. To thoroughly explore improvisation in music would fill a whole book, and indeed there are many! There are some tips, though, that these improvisational greats can impart to musicians who are starting out on their career in music.

Improvisation in general is strongly linked to practising your craft and honing your skills. Being the person who is a 'master' in improvisation is often in demand on all kinds of records, as demonstrated for example by Bernard Purdie, Tal Wilkenfeld, Nile

Rodgers, Blake Mills, Hal Blaine, Steve Lukather and Carol Kaye. They are constantly working and are in such high demand, largely because their musicianship gives them the ability to improvise on a completely different level from that of many other players.

Above all, improvisation is about staying flexible and being OK with surprises, and that is an excellent life lesson too. You don't have to be a music expert to improvise, but tapping into your message and accurately expressing how you feel is what makes improvising a great skill.

At its most basic level, you should be able to hear when a tune doesn't sound right or is out of key. Jamming and collaborating with friends is also a super-fun way to develop your improvising skills. Whether in hustling or performing, taking lessons or joining workshops led by experienced musicians can give you great tips and feedback, allowing you to improve your improvising in both life and musical situations.

It takes time to get good at improvising and hustling, but on all levels there's only so much talking about it you can do. Get out there and see what happens, both on the stage and in the meeting room. It pays to be patient with yourself and practise these skills regularly. The more you explore your openness, the more that will give you the ability to adapt.

TRY THIS NOW: Finding your authentic self in sound

What chord represents how you feel now? Try to find it, and play it. This is about keeping yourself absolutely and completely in the moment.

Can you do this with notes? Can you do this with solos? Maybe you can do this with ideas or venues or fees?

All too easily, we can get caught in patterns and loops. We forever associate this or that venue or this or that scale or this or that solo with this or that emotion.

Try to undo the damage, to break free from those patterns. What is your state of mind now? Perform and speak from that place, not from the past and not from what you've learned or what should be correct or what you want from the future.

The more you can groove in the 'eternal now', the better the performer (and hustler) you will be.

Steve Berry: Open your mind, open your ears

Steve Berry, born in the UK on 24 August 1957, is well-known name in the world of jazz. A virtuoso jazz double bassist, composer and educator, his journey into music was far from conventional. His story begins not in a traditional music school but during his pursuit of a fine art degree. It was here that his fascination with jazz first sparked. In 1979, under the guidance of jazz legends like Chris Laurence, Daryl Runswick and Dave Holland, he honed his craft and deepened his passion for the genre. By 1984 Steve had joined the influential jazz ensemble Loose Tubes, a move that marked the beginning of his career as both a performer and a composer. In 1988 he formed his own trio, the Steve Berry Trio, which released an album under the Loose Tubes record label.

Throughout his career, Steve has collaborated with some of jazz's finest talents: Scott Hamilton, John Surman, Tal Farlow and Art Farmer, to name just a few. His versatility has made him a sought-after musician, respected not only for his playing but also for his deep understanding of improvisation and expressing himself in the moment. In 2019 he took on a new role as head of jazz and improvisation at the Royal Northern College of Music, and he continues to inspire young musicians at the renowned Chetham's School of Music.

Recently, I had the chance to sit down with Steve and discuss his musical journey and what he believes is the key to becoming a successful musician. Reflecting on his path, Steve explained that to understand how he teaches and approaches music, I'd need to know where he started. In the beginning he was a self-taught singer-songwriter – no sheet music, simply learning by ear and copying from records. He remembers the thrill of finding a new chord shape and how amazing it sounded. When that happened, he thought he was discovering music for the first time, but he suddenly realised there was a whole world of music theory he didn't even know existed.

Steve's early experiences were marked by a reluctance to see himself as a student, admitting that it took him a long time to adopt the humility that comes with that. For Steve that was a hard lesson, but it was one that changed his perspective on learning and teaching. He says he always tells his students that they are already ahead of where he was when he started. The fact that they've chosen to study music, that they've signed up to go to college, shows they've already taken a huge step. Then when they say, 'Help me with this', it's a powerful thing. Steve found it hard to admit that he didn't have all the answers, but once he did, he began to grow as a musician and as a teacher.

One of the most important messages Steve imparts to his students is about accepting where they are right now in their musical journey: 'A huge part of my work always is to encourage the person who's playing to embrace the vocabulary they have at this moment – embrace it, enjoy it, welcome it – and then develop a healthy attitude towards developing and extending it.'

For many students, he said, this is one of the hardest lessons to learn, and musicians too often get discouraged. They compare themselves to others and think, *I'll never be as good as him or her*. That mindset is the biggest obstacle, though. Music isn't about competition, Steve explained. It's about learning to hear – truly listen to the possibilities around you.

It's this openness to discovery, this willingness to embrace the moment and to learn from every experience, that has defined Steve Berry's career.

> Whether as a performer, a composer or a teacher, he has always been about one thing: pushing the boundaries of what is possible through music, and sharing that joy with others.
>
> You can hear the full interview with Steve on my *More in the Moni* podcast at www.moreinthemoni.com.

The value of the small venue

If you're new to playing music in front of people, it's vital you start doing it as soon as you can. When I deliver workshops, I always tell students that most of what I teach in the classroom can be learned far more quickly by actually performing in an open mic event just a couple of times or by putting on your own show. Talking about it, studying it or imagining it is good for some things, but it won't help much. You have to get out there and face the fear.

When I'm getting ready for a tour, I always go and play it in a bar in front of a small audience, purely because of the value that gives me in terms of accurate and focused rehearsal. Many times I realise I didn't know a whole verse, or I messed up the chorus and other parts, but that's OK – it's all part of learning. I recommend that bands should get their set lists together and then immediately book a gig. Don't wait around for it to be perfect in a practice room, because it never will be. You'll find as soon as you do the gig that all kinds of things go wrong, so it's healthy to get all of that out of the system early on.

Doing gigs in small venues also allows you to meet new people, make relationships with promoters, do some genuine networking and maybe even begin to develop a fanbase. Artists like Ed Sheeran are famous for this exact work ethic: treading the boards in as many small venues as possible.

> **Paul Jones: From fan to director of The Cavern**
>
> I first met Paul in the streets of Liverpool. I was about five years old, riding bikes and skateboards with my mates, carefree and wild. Paul was one of those kids, always ready for adventure. As we grew older, we swapped the BMX bikes and park swings for something that would define the rest of our lives: music.
>
> Paul's musical journey is intertwined with one of the world's most iconic venues, The Cavern Club. It was there that Paul, at the age of sixteen, took his first steps onto the stage, performing with his band. Not long after, the band made an appearance on the UK show *Stars In Their Eyes*, and Paul's taste of TV fame helped kickstart his career.
>
> His ambition took him further and further, from the stage of *The X Factor* to the halls of the Liverpool Institute for Performing Arts (LIPA). It was here that he honed his skills, and soon after graduating, Paul was off on a whirlwind tour, performing Beatles

tribute shows around the globe – Japan, China, Australia, the USA, Brazil and just about anywhere else you can think of.

In 2011 Paul returned to his roots in Liverpool, joining The Cavern Club Beatles, the club's resident tribute band. Paul took on the role of George Harrison, and the band quickly became renowned for their authentic renditions of Beatles songs. They still perform every Saturday, keeping the spirit of the Fab Four alive for fans from all over the world.

Today Paul is one of the directors of the Cavern business and works tirelessly behind the scenes with Cavern City Tours. He manages the entertainment schedule and plays a key role in organising the annual International Beatleweek festival.

He recalls that he started like any kid, picking up a guitar and forming a little school band. They learned a few Beatles songs, and before they knew it, they got booked for their first gig at a wedding in Kirkby. After that, they thought, *How can we turn this £50 into £60, then £70?* He says that's when the hunger to grow started.

Paul's journey is a testament to his love for The Beatles and Liverpool's rich musical heritage, but also to the power of hustling and 'seeing what happens'. He's made incredible strides and continues to make a major impact on the music scene in every way he can.

You can hear the full interview with Paul and his co-director, John Keats, on my *More in the Moni* podcast at www.moreinthemoni.com.

When you're performing or hustling, you may find things difficult at first. Even if you only say, *Hi, my name is X, and I've never done this before, but I'm gonna do my best*, you're much more likely to get the audience and promoters on side, you're more likely to focus yourself more, and you'll realise that they're not as scary as you might have thought. Connect with them. It's all about staying calm and enjoying the experience, as opposed to the gig setting you up for a fall.

I find that managing nerves, including implementing relaxation techniques like deep breathing or visualisation, is mostly a waste of time. You're going to feel terrified, and that's a fact, especially if it's your first gig. In some ways that adrenaline of wondering how many tickets you've sold doesn't go away, even when you're selling thousands. Don't run away from that fact; simply accept it and go with the situation as it unfolds. Embrace the adrenaline as it hits you, because it can actually enhance your energy when you finally get on the stage. Simply tell your audience, whoever they may be, that you're nervous – they'll love you for it.

Handling mistakes gracefully is part of a professional performance. If any mistakes occur, don't worry about it. Remember that most of the room can't or won't ever do whatever you're doing. Being on a stage or hustling for work frightens most people, so the very fact that you're up there doing it should say something really positive about you. Stay composed and continue confidently. Also, don't forget to thank people and make them feel appreciated – audience, promoters or otherwise.

TRY THIS NOW: Handling mistakes

Record your next performance, particularly the improvised segments, and engage afterwards in some reflective analysis. Identify successful elements, challenges and audience responses for continuous growth and refinement of improvisational skills.

Try to see areas where you could've been more relaxed or fostered spontaneous interactions between band members, and so on, allowing for unexpected musical cues, call-and-response dynamics, or impromptu jam sessions that evolved organically.

How do you handle mistakes? What could you do to define them as interesting rather than as errors?

Enhancing your live performance

Performing live is awesome. Record companies and fans want your live music to sound just as good as the songs you've recorded in the studio. If you want to impress people and make your music sound exactly like the recording, there's an important thing you must do: have separate music parts, called *stems*, to play during your performance.

In live performance, stems are separate audio tracks or parts of a song that are isolated from each other. These stems typically include individual elements of the music, like vocals, drums, guitar, bass and other instruments. Musicians use stems to have more control over their live sound. You can get your producer to print your stems once you have them recorded in a studio.

Incorporating backing tracks and stems into your live performances involves several key steps, the first two being:

1. Assess which musical elements need backing tracks. These could be things like orchestral arrangements, electronic sounds, vocal harmonies or complex synths.

2. Choose the songs from your repertoire where these additional elements would make a big impact.

Collaborating with great producers or arrangers can create top-notch backing stems that match your artistic vibe. You have to make sure that the production enhances your music while keeping its essence intact – you don't want to merely play the audience a Spotify mix. The point of stems is that they're there to enhance something that's already good. You can create separate stems for each musical element in the tracks, and these stems help control each part during the live show. If you watch more theatrical performances by the likes of Billie Eilish, Lady Gaga, Michael Jackson, Bruno Mars, etc, you'll see that stems will often be used to introduce songs, transition one song to another, or add sound effects that you simply wouldn't be able to recreate using normal instruments.

Because stems are so important for levelling up your performance, you'll have to invest in reliable playback systems like laptops or dedicated devices, and test them thoroughly to avoid technical issues. Plan ahead, with backup systems and copies of tracks in case of emergencies!

The use of stems means devoting more time to sound checks and rehearsals with the backing tracks to find the right balance between live instruments and backing elements. Equip yourself and your band with in-ear monitoring systems (IEMs) to hear the tracks clearly. The costs of IEMs are on a sliding scale, with prices ranging between £200 and £4k.

It can be great fun to map out smooth transitions between live and backing sections, and you need to practise these switches until they feel natural. It's all about giving you the opportunity to engage with the audience while using backing tracks. You have to be ready to adapt to unexpected situations like technical problems or venue changes. Incorporating stems into your live performances provides an extra-exciting and immersive musical experience for your audience, so don't forget to check it out.

Performing live is increasingly becoming the primary way for musicians to make good money, and live music significantly contributes to the economy. Given the challenges we face around streaming and AI, it's essential to work on your live show and make that human connection with paying fans who've bought tickets to come and see you perform.

SIX
Grow Your Community And Scale It Up

A major factor contributing to the success and viability of any musician is their community. This isn't about appealing to the mass market or to the world, and it's not about burning yourself out trying to please everybody. It's about appealing to *your* market – the one you've created. This chapter explores the value of social media, growing your community and how to scale it up.

Embracing social media

I've noticed that a lot of musicians don't really like using social media. You'd be surprised how many artists aren't in fact extroverts; they are quite the opposite and are rather nervous, pensive beings. Maybe they're too focused on their music or think they're 'too cool' for socials. If you want to become popular, though, you need to use social media. You could be the Lord God himself, but unless your TikTok numbers or Instagram reels are making good impressions, you ain't lord of anything. Seriously, our society is that extreme!

If you want to be paid for playing gigs and get great opportunities, you need to show that you have lots of fans, or at the very least that the fans you do have are loyal and engaged. The quickest and easiest way to check that is – you guessed it – through the internet. Even if you're super-talented, if your numbers on TikTok or other sites aren't impressive, people won't perceive you as an artist to be taken seriously. In short, even if you don't like social media, it's just one of those shit sandwiches you're gonna have to swallow.

As I emphasised in Chapter Two, it's important to know who you are as a musician. Your music style and, yes, your social media presence depend on that. If your social media profiles don't have a clear personality, direction, message or something to share or sell, it's difficult to convert people over to real fandom. That's because today is all about the battle of attention spans.

There exists a fierce battle for attention in the online community. A staggering 200 million creators compete for their digital foothold, navigating the challenge of capturing and retaining their audience's engagement. This minefield of content creation leaves both creators and viewers wading through a never-ending avalanche.

Recent research on US teenagers showed that nearly half of girls (45%) say they feel overwhelmed by the drama on social media, compared with just over a third (32%) of boys.[2] Girls are also more likely than boys to feel excluded by their friends because of social media (37% vs 24%) or to say it has made them feel worse about their own lives (28% vs 18%). Statistically speaking, according to studies, the human attention span has dropped. According to Golden Steps, 'The average attention span of an adult is 8 seconds, which is one second less than a goldfish' and, 'In 2000, the average attention span of an adult was 12 seconds, meaning it has decreased by a whopping 33% in just two decades.'[3]

The remedy doesn't lie in creating more content. It lies in crafting your online presence and drawing it all together in a single theme or story with a single message.

While powerhouse platforms like Instagram, YouTube and TikTok hold sway, harmonising your content and consolidating it all in the one place enables cross-discovery, allowing your Instagram followers to stumble on your podcast, book or album release. This is the value of a great website; or of a Linktree (https://linktr.ee), which attracts over three times the views per visitor each month. Letting your fans know where they can find everything is extremely powerful.

Spotify advises you to release music every six weeks, while Instagram recommends you post four or five times a week. Adhering solely to algorithmic preferences, though, often leads to a monotonous cycle of content repetition, on the whole polluting the internet with the same old stuff.

In a world where attention is scarce and time all-important, first impressions reign supreme. Creators are the very essence of their brand. Their message and their story are what they're selling. Diversifying revenue streams only draws their audience closer.

TRY THIS NOW: Social media decisions

Get yourself the social media apps and platforms you think are most relevant to you and your message.

Jot down some initial ideas about the platforms themselves – the messages that they're specifically designed to convey and the audience they're trying to convey it to.

Will Hooley: Embracing social media as a positive tool

Will Hooley is best known for his time as a fly-half with the San Diego Legion in Major League Rugby (MLR) and the United States national team. His rugby career spanned multiple clubs, including Northampton Saints, Exeter Chiefs, Saracens and Bedford Blues, and he represented his country at various age/grade levels, contributing to England's victory in the 2013 IRB Junior World Championship.

After retiring from rugby, Will transitioned into media, becoming a prominent writer for publications such as *The Guardian* and *The Observer* in the UK. He has also embraced roles in podcasting and journalism, and he has developed a notable media presence. I had the opportunity to chat with Will about his journey, and he shared some insightful thoughts on how social media has played a crucial role in his career transition.

He explained that social media has been incredibly beneficial for him, saying that in today's world it's vital to your personal brand – ultimately, it helps you sell yourself. Will said that rugby is a traditional sport, where the idea of athletes expressing their personalities in front of a camera wasn't always embraced, but that's changing. When he spent time in California, he saw how American sports celebrate individual characters, especially in the NFL. Social media allows you to present yourself beyond simply being 'Will Hooley, the rugby player', he said. It lets people see who you really are, and what you're passionate about outside of the sport.

> Will told me he'd always wanted to be involved in media, to share his story and his experience. Social media has therefore been a free advertising tool for him – through his podcast, writing blogs and sharing his journey – an essential platform for building his profile and gaining experience. Will said he's proud to say that he's already successfully transitioned out of professional sport and into his next career in media, particularly in the US, and social media played a huge role in that. He used it to build his presence, get noticed and connect with people.
>
> Will maintains that social media isn't only about gaining fame or attention; when used properly, it's a fantastic tool for engaging with your audience, expressing yourself and building your own brand. It's about being authentic and showcasing the real you. While his presence is on a smaller scale compared with some big names, there's no doubt it's been hugely beneficial for him, and he says he's convinced that anyone can use it to their advantage.
>
> You can hear the full interview on my *More in the Moni* podcast at www.moreinthemoni.com.

For a lot of artists, the idea of being on the internet feels overwhelming. Many new musicians I talk to don't really care about their social media and shun it, saying that they're 'real' musicians, uninterested in all of that. All that confirms about them is a lack of awareness of the times, a complete disregard for what fans want (and for where the fans are) and a genuine desire to alienate themselves from what would or could be a positive and engaging community of supporters. Usually, these concerns come primarily from not truly understanding how social media works, thinking too much about it, or secretly being jealous of people with big numbers and not being able to achieve them.

Backlinko reports that 'More than half (55%) of TikTok weekly active users in the US are between 18 and 34', and 'US adult users spend an average of 53.8 minutes per day on TikTok'.[4] According to BusinessDasher, 'On average, Instagram users spend about 29.2 minutes per day scrolling through the app, engaging with content, and connecting with others. Remarkably, 63% of Instagram users log in at least once daily to check the app.'[5]

There's no doubt that social media plays a huge role in people's lives across the globe. If you're not on there because of fear of change or fear of failure, then you're simply not being seen. The crux of why some on social media are successful and others aren't lies in the focus on creating content that resonates with you *and* your audience, not merely on pleasing algorithms.

Making social media work for you

Building a strong presence online involves lots of steps, but there's one all-important thing that many artists forget about at the start: personality. This all comes back to owning your message. Once you get this, every post and video you share online becomes a chance to tell that message to the world.

Making money from social media is an achievable goal. When you fully understand your message, you can put all your energy into being online. Your fans aren't only a big group; they're unique people with different tastes and feelings.

Some people will hate everything you do. That's fine. Treat them with respect and say *Thanks very much*. You can't be liked by everybody, and you don't need to be. Building an online presence means setting clear goals. Just saying *I want ten million followers* isn't helpful. You need to think about what you can and want to realistically achieve. Start off with these questions:

- Is there something you want to sell?
- Do you only need the numbers to get into a deal?
- Do you want a great community?

A small group of dedicated fans, who look forward to seeing your beautiful posts and who are impelled to buy your tickets or engage with your content, is a strong benchmark to lead with.

The key to social media is understanding it. A big part of getting to grips with social media is understanding that the internet is like a living system with machines, with rules by robots (called algorithms) on one hand and people on the other. Those people all benefit from what the algorithms deem important to prioritise and from what the mass psychology of human beings think is really shareable.

For example, when you post something on social media, if those posts do well and manage to get engagement, it makes the robots (algorithms) notice you more, which in turn prioritises that post and places it in more visible spots to be shown to a much greater audience. Active participation is therefore the key factor that makes the computer systems prioritise us and our posts, which gets our content to more people.

On one hand, we need to know what the algorithms like and what they look for. Crucially, though, as well as appealing to the robots, we need to satisfy what human beings like to see as well. You need content that's genuinely interesting and engaging for people (actual, real human beings), and you need to post it in such a way that you trigger robotic algorithmic preferences too.

Algorithms continuously evolve, and it's worth looking online to keep in touch with the latest tricks to increase your social media presence. Quite simply, though, the robots of all social media of any kind all like it best when you use their platform. That means that when you like, share and comment, and when you are in turn liked, shared and commented on, the robots recognise that your account should be given priority, because you are generating engagement and shareability, not only for yourself but also for the platform.

Breaking some myths and maximising engagement

Social media success isn't all about trends, expensive production or high post frequency. It's about authenticity, engagement and execution. Stick to your message, connect with your audience and let your expertise shine through – not your desperation or your 'sales technique'. Here are six myths that most musicians should steer clear of when they're getting started:

- Myth 1: It's all about pleasing everyone
- Myth 2: I have to post frequently
- Myth 3: I have to go with trends
- Myth 4: I need expensive cameras and equipment
- Myth 5: I need to be on every platform
- Myth 6: I need to sell myself

Myth 1: It's all about pleasing everyone

Switch from a one-to-million mindset to a one-to-one mindset.

Social media isn't about broadcasting to the masses of people who are generally uninterested in what you do – it's about connecting with *individuals*. Getting a comment or like from twenty of your friends is far more powerful than getting no interest from everyone in the Western Hemisphere. Engagement is key. Every post should feel personal, relatable and designed to spark a response.

Ask yourself the following, making notes as you progress:

- How can I make my content interactive?
- How do my posts invite conversation, reaction, or action?

Myth 2: I have to post frequently

Many hugely successful content creators like Mr Beast, T-Series, Khaby Lame and Amelia Dimoldenberg often take a huge amount of time creating great content, sometimes meaning they can only post once a month! That's because they know that posting often doesn't guarantee success.

Key tips to remember:

- Instead of focusing on volume and frequency, prioritise consistency and post when you have something valuable to share.

- Prioritise authenticity by creating content that resonates, not purely with the aim of filling space.

Myth 3: I have to go with trends

Trends can be helpful and interesting for the odd quirky post, but on the whole they don't matter. Jumping on every trend can dilute your brand. The best content stands out because it's different, not because it follows the crowd.

You need to:

- Ignore the trends and focus on your message.
- Stay true to your expertise and uniqueness.

Myth 4: I need expensive cameras and equipment

Production value doesn't equal success. High-end production is nice, but execution is what matters. The quality required depends on what you're trying to create and the message you're trying to demonstrate, but great content can be filmed on a phone if the message is strong.

Before worrying about cameras and lighting and making expensive (and unsustainable) posts, ask yourself the following:

- Is my content authentic and engaging?
- Does my content serve my audience and my brand's message?

Myth 5: I need to be on every platform

How can you be engaging if you don't really like social media *and* you're trying to be everywhere all at once? You don't have to be on every social media platform – the key is in choosing the right platform for *you*.

Pick the ones that match:

- The resources you have (eg phone, camera, editing skills)
- The content you enjoy creating
- Where your audience seems to be most active

Myth 6: I need to sell myself

Selling yourself or your products can only do so much. Sometimes it's relevant to let people know where to buy an album or a T-shirt, but audiences quickly get tired of constantly being persuaded to like something. People engage with experts, not advertisements. Would you go out with someone just because they relentlessly kept asking you? No – you'd do the opposite.

Here are the key points to focus on:

- Show your expertise and authenticity rather than only selling things.
- Instead of pushing products, focus on sharing insights and experience, educating your audience and providing real and authentic value to your fans.
- Provide insights and behind-the-scenes, personalised tips and content.
- Celebrate your audience, not you.

The phases of marketing

There is a tonne of advice out there on social media strategy, but a lot of it can be reduced to four key phases. They are:

- Phase 1: Research
- Phase 2: Growth
- Phase 3: Engagement

Phase 1: Research

The main goal on your social media is to show who you are and what your message is. At the beginning, don't waste money on hiring someone to run all of this for you. Your first job is to figure out how to share your message using pictures and videos. This doesn't cost money – it only needs a bit of time, patience and thinking about yourself:

- Who are you?
- What do you want?
- What are you trying to say?
- Is that clear on your profile?

Planning what to share and keeping that consistent is super-important for connecting with your audience. Create content that goes with your brand and makes sense to the people you want to reach.

Don't be someone who says they're one thing but acts differently. Don't try to get everyone's attention; instead, focus on the people who are already looking for someone like you. Whoever you truly are, that's what you need to show and celebrate. When you fully embrace who you are, both online and offline, you don't need to pretend. When you understand your message and who you are, the hard part is done. If people see your profile and it doesn't seem real, they won't follow you. Being real is more important than having perfect pictures and videos.

Once you've done your research and figured out what you want your brand to be about, the next important thing is choosing a good name and handle (the @name on your socials) for your account. There are plenty of examples that illustrate that this isn't super-important, but it helps to have a name that's unique and easy to say, or a handle that's snappy and to the point. Your handle won't be memorable if it looks like a Wi-Fi password. Personally, I would avoid handles that look something like @_the. winter-band821 and go for something shorter and snappier like @ye.

Choosing names and brands

Sometimes, using your own name is OK, as demonstrated by Ed Sheeran or Dua Lipa. You might have the same name as someone well known, though, so you might need to choose a different name to make a distinction from others or stand out. In those cases, there are different ways to think about picking the right name.

Common attributes among human beings manifest in our language, thoughts and actions. Harsher, guttural sounds often represent strength, while softer sounds indicate weakness. It's no coincidence that characters like the Devil, Diablo, Darth Vader, Count Dracula, Archangel Gabriel, Gandhi, Nobunaga, Voldemort, Adolf Hitler and Yoda – all with hard vocal sounds – hold significant places in our minds, whether they are fearsome or benevolent. It's also not surprising that a growth mindset is universally embraced as a sign of healthy mental activity. Guitarists, being the cool ones in bands, may follow a similar pattern!

I argue that artists or actors with names containing harder vowel sounds tend to fare better because they are more memorable or significant to us than those without them. Examples include Bruce Lee, Leonardo DiCaprio, Brad Pitt, Johnny Depp, Beyoncé, Ariana Grande, One Direction, Diplo, Dua Lipa, Bastille, Bob Marley, and The Beatles. The same principle applies to company names like Google, Adidas, Colt, Puma, Bentley, Lamborghini, Blizzard, Betfred, Burger King, and McDonald's.

My first name, Ben (with a hard b sound), sticks in people's memories, while my last name, Hughes, is often misspelled or forgotten. My own artist name, Hughzy, came about simply because enough people were calling me that without my influence, so it simply stuck. It also has a slightly scouse feel (I'm from Liverpool) and is spelled in an unusual way. Had it not been the case, I might've gone with something more guttural. It's not surprising that words like *gold bricks*, *cash*, *credit card* and *consciousness* (with hard g, b, c sounds) convey concrete ideas of wealth or health and are easily remembered. On the other hand, words like *money*, *change*, *stock*, *wealth*, *success* and *enlightenment* are more abstract and subject to lots of debate.

If you're choosing your artist name, the name of your band or brand, opt for sounds like c/k, b, d, g, t, p.

Psychologically, they tend to convey bigness, goodness and positivity, and they are generally more memorable than softer sounds like ch, j, sh, l.

Phase 2: Growth

In this growth phase you're after four main goals:

- Brand awareness
- Algorithmic recognition (using bots)
- Word-of-mouth
- Leveraging your friends and connections

This phase involves creating and launching campaigns. It also means keeping an eye on things, using analytics and understanding the data you receive. While you're doing all this, it's crucial to watch closely, track the important numbers and make sure you're moving in the direction you planned.

Steering the herd

The growth phase breaks down like this. You want to be paying for strategic, well-calculated and tightly budgeted growth via the use of ads, hooks and some legitimate marketing for little to no money, while at the same time absolutely hammering your message in a strictly confined or even non-existent spend.

The psychology of human beings is such that you if you go to a venue and hear the best music on the planet but the room is empty, your brain instantly tells you the music can't be very good. Conversely, if you go to a venue where the music is dreadful, as long as it's packed out and everybody is talking about it and having fun, you're much more likely to try to stick around and find out what all the fuss is about. This herd mentality applies to social media posting and chart success alike. Some of the worst music in history has done brilliantly well because someone had the foresight to quickly grow the accounts or the following of the artist. They knew that people will largely go with the herd and get behind anything as long as their friends are doing the same. Some artists are never off the radio, but it's often not because their song is any better than yours. It's more likely that someone is financing that song to position it again and again, knowing that eventually, because everyone's always hearing it, it will be perceived to be a success.

Picture this: I tell you about a new band. You ask who they are, I show you their Instagram page, and you see it has no followers. Do you want to listen to the music? Almost certainly not. Psychologically, something happens to us when a page is barren.

Now picture this: I tell you about a new band. Their Instagram page has a few thousand followers and the content is strong, thematised and consistent with the message. They're also doing legitimate gigs and selling out small-capacity venues on a bimonthly basis, and they can be seen in a local pub playing some stripped back covers on a Tuesday. That's something you, I, A&R, managers and bloggers will all be interested in. The point of social media is not to be an accountable lie detector – it's a promotional tool, and it's all about telling a story that's authentically your own. As long as you're constantly guiding your fans to the *next* thing – events, launches of a new EP, new badges for sale, a support tour, etc – you're doing great.

I recommend you avoid spending too much on ads. You could, say, post a video that gets only three likes, but then you pay for ads and it suddenly gets 300 likes. That initial boost might seem great at first, but unless you follow up by consistently delivering valuable content, you'll have to keep spending money on ads to maintain the illusion that your account is doing well. Regular interaction and engagement with your audience are what turn your followers from mere numbers into genuine, interested fans. Paid promotions can serve as a catalyst to kickstart this process, but the ongoing quality of your content and interactions is what sustains it.

Phase 3: Engagement

Engagement is about how your fans connect with you. Do they like your posts and leave comments? Do they bring their friends to your page? When they visit your account, do they buy things or only scroll through?

It's important to understand these behaviours and why they happen.

Relationship building

To do well in marketing in the long term, you need to make strong connections with your customers. This means you need to keep talking to them, understand what they want and make them like your brand. Here are some ways to do that:

- Create online forms, chatrooms, and Facebook, WhatsApp or Snapchat groups. These will enable you to build loyalty and longevity, and people will trust you more.

- When people write reviews or comments online, make sure you answer them quickly and nicely. If someone says something bad, deal with it well so people still like your brand.

- Keep talking to your followers, and ask them for thoughts and advice. Get them to join discussions. This helps your brand get closer to your fans.

- Stay connected by sending them emails, but don't send too many. You can send them cool stuff like content, deals, news and updates. This keeps your fans interested and informed.

- Make sure your brand looks the same on every website. This helps people trust you more.

- Be on social media where it makes sense for your brand and where you can share the right message. Remember that you don't have to be everywhere, and it's difficult to manage a presence on absolutely every platform. If you're a singer, you'll want to be on platforms for videos like TikTok or YouTube. There will be no benefit from posting pictures or daily thoughts, for example on Pinterest or X. If you're an artist with content that is particularly relevant for X, like James Blunt, then go ahead – get an X account and start the convo!

If you do all this with the correct message, consistency and quality of content, you will see your channels increase. It's that simple.

> **Tracey Webb: The power of consistent content**
>
> Tracey Webb, a key player in the music industry, is the owner and music executive of Power Promotions. With a career spanning over three decades, she has worked alongside global artists like Calvin Harris, Ella Henderson, Faithless, Craig David, Sigma, Becky Hill, David Guetta, Jonas Blue, Charli XCX, Jazzy, Nathan Dawe, Rudimental, Galantis, Tiësto, Sigala... and the list goes on.
>
> Her company Power is the UK's leading dance music promotions company. Having been around since the birth of dance music, Power has unparalleled

expertise in promoting the world's biggest club tracks. Tracey's journey began humbly at CD Pool, where she handled CD packing and office tasks. Her passion for music quickly propelled her into the spotlight, where she helped shape the direction of music promotion while collaborating with top record labels such as Atlantic Records, Ministry of Sound, Columbia Records, Positiva Records and Black Butter Records.

Tracey's ability to spot the right songs for the right moments, combined with her extensive industry knowledge, has been crucial to the success of both major and independent artists. Her approach is defined by her willingness to say no when a song doesn't align with the artist's vision, maintaining a clear sense of direction and purpose.

In a recent podcast conversation, Tracey shared some important and insightful tips for aspiring artists. She emphasised the importance of constantly creating and sharing music, staying true to yourself, and giving it your all in the ever-evolving digital landscape. Here's Tracey's advice on entering the world of signed artists:

'I would say a constant flow of music – don't take your eye off the ball; don't have a gap. With the digital world that we're in now, it's very easy to release music. You just need an aggregator now.'

Tracey added that you can use companies such as CD Baby or AWAL, where you can upload your music yourself, and you can have a release yourself. You don't need to pay stupid amounts for a distributor like you used to have to do: 'I would just say keep the content coming, push on the social medias, keep the releases coming, upload them. If you don't want to put them on Spotify with an aggregator like I suggested, get them on SoundCloud and then post, post, post on your social media links to it.'

Tracey says that if your song contains a sample of another artist, then tag that other artist. It's about the numbers and keeping the flow of the music coming. It's not easy, but to get on people's radar, there's got to be a bit of heat: 'You've got to do something! You can't just have a record that's cold.'

Tracey's profound influence on the music industry reflects her passion and dedication, and her exceptional talent for connecting huge teams of people to create something truly special.

Visit Power's website at www.power.co.uk.

Don't miss my full interview with Tracey on my *More in the Moni* podcast at www.moreinthemoni.com.

Social media is now key to how we promote ourselves and consume products and brands. Learning how to tell an engaging story through the mediums that social media offer can be the difference between success and failure for many musicians.

SEVEN
Get A Team

By now you're realising that there's a lot to do in the music industry and that it's hard to sustain it all, let alone finance everything by yourself. That's why you need a great team to help you along the way. The art of getting a great team together, no matter who it is on the whole, is in being able to prove to them that you not only can talk the talk, but you can also very much walk the walk.

Most of my life, and most of what I do now at Cherry Up Projects, is all about assembling and coordinating teams of people, managing the dynamics, and delegating the jobs within that team. That's even on my own tours! Sometimes a team will be a band, a management group, a marketing agency; it could be just about anything. Delegating and organising a great team takes work, but it is absolutely essential. Fortunately, I've found myself to be rather good at that, making it something I consider to be an area of my specialism.

Team members for a musician can be pretty much anyone you can think of that helps delegate or offset some of the workload, including:

- Managers
- Songwriters
- Vocal coaches
- Agents
- Promoters
- Friends
- Parents
- Security guards
- Investors
- Labels
- Chefs
- Drivers
- Marketing gurus

This chapter explores the value of a team and how to attract one.

Why you need a team

Imagine playing for a professional football team, then on match day you were the only person that turned up, and you had to single-handedly beat Liverpool FC. You couldn't, could you? That's because the team is stronger than the player. Every time you go for a strike, you leave the goal completely empty; and whenever you go to defend your goal, you're not putting any moves out there to strike with.

A team covers your bases. It increases your strategic power and your ability to sustain what you're doing. Without a team, you'll end up running all over the pitch in every direction until you collapse.

The quality of your team is now even factored into pitch meetings. If you're an artist doing everything by yourself, at some point someone in the meeting will ask, *Why don't they have a team of people?* Not having a team usually signals that there's something wrong. Others will think, *If they're that good, why does nobody want to work with them?*

Conversely, if you have a great team of people, with credibility and a track record, this can greatly accentuate your viability and opportunities with labels, agent deals and even investors or promoters.

Lorna Blackwood: The beauty of self-discovery

Lorna Blackwood's name is synonymous with vocal excellence. Her roster of clients reads like a Who's Who of international pop stars: George Ezra, Tom Walker, Dua Lipa, Ellie Goulding, Frank Carter, Mabel, Beabadoobee, Calum Scott – artists whose voices have shaped the modern music scene. Behind every note they sing is Lorna's expertise in vocal production and coaching, helping these artists discover their fullest potential, both on stage and in the studio.

Her career didn't start with A-list names and Grammy-winning albums. It began in the world of musical theatre, where Lorna's passion for vocals led her to study at the Arts Educational London Schools. Her heart wasn't only in acting, though – it was in singing, and after transitioning to gigging and songwriting, she found her true calling as a vocal coach.

From her early work with George Ezra on his breakthrough album, *Wanted On Voyage*, to her pivotal role in Dua Lipa's *Future Nostalgia* (which won a Grammy for Best Pop Vocal Album), Lorna's approach to vocal coaching has been a revelation. She doesn't only teach technique; she helps each artist connect deeply with their voice, nurturing their unique sound and guiding them through the complexities of the music industry.

Dua Lipa is even reported to have joked that all it takes to keep her voice in top shape is 'Honey, lemons and Lorna'.

It's Lorna's personalised coaching, tailored to each artist's personality, that sets her apart. Whether she's preparing singers for a high-stakes TV performance or helping them maintain vocal health during a gruelling tour, Lorna's methods are all about longevity and sustainable success.

She explains that it's not enough to just show up anymore. Touring schedules are packed, and there's so much more to juggle: promo, social media, interviews. It's no longer possible to be the 'wild child' and have a long career.

What makes Lorna's work truly special, though, is her understanding of something that's often overlooked in the rush for fame and success: self-discovery. She sees it as one of the most beautiful aspects of an artist's journey: 'Especially with really young artists or artists that are new to the music industry, there is an element of self-discovery.'

Lorna says that those artists are figuring out who they are, both as people and as musicians. It's a challenging process, but it's also incredible. Fans get to watch this evolution, and it's such a powerful thing to be part of.

Lorna understands not only the beauty of self-discovery but also the importance of the team taking on the heavy lifting so the artist doesn't have to, allowing them the space they need.

You can listen to the full interview with Lorna on my *More in the Moni* podcast at www.moreinthemoni.com.

How to create a team

The word that constantly comes up when discussing team building is *networking*. Though it is undoubtedly a huge factor in you being able to increase your team, networking needs to be done in the right way if it is to be of any value.

I always shudder when I'm invited to standard networking events. They may be great if you're a mortgage salesman or a dentist, but my experience of forced networking in the music industry is very negative.

For me valuable networking really means getting to know someone who can assist you. This often fails at standard networking events because the other person is either not interested in knowing you or just can't help you (or both!). The difficulties in navigating the nuances of networking should not undermine the actual real-world value of what it's genuinely all about, though.

Networking is a lot easier for a musician than for people in other jobs. As a musician, most of what you do naturally demands that you go and hang out in places where people are having fun. Networking places can include open mics, pubs, bars, local gigs, your own gigs, cafés, clubs, raves, pool parties – essentially, any venue you can think of.

When you go out with the agenda of meeting someone, it works like trying to get a date: it never happens if you try too hard. You won't make any sincere connections if you view people merely as contacts, and you won't be able to get any meaningful team members on the basis of *What can you do for me?*

What networking should accomplish

Networking can mean many different things, including:

- Going to events such as workshops or industry-related gatherings where you can meet others

- Being friendly and starting conversations with people who have similar interests

- Swapping contact info with anyone you meet so you can stay in touch

- Using the internet, especially sites like LinkedIn

If you go to too many networking events, you can burn yourself out and be seen as too easy. If you don't go to enough or to the right ones, though, you won't get yourself out there. Good networking all comes down to what you intend to accomplish and why. Obviously you want to get further and get contacts, but to what end, and where are you planning on getting those contacts?

At the start, an artist project needs the following key network and team members:

- **Great artists:** The best artists to partner up with will be talented and have no problem creating music and content. They should be consistent, talented, knowledgeable about the industry, road tested at least with their local scene and active on social media. They should possibly also have some basic production skills.

- **Producer:** This needs to be someone who can record the music well enough. This person could change over time if the project requires it, but you need someone who can produce a great concept initially.

- **Manager:** You want a manager who can keep their eye on the future and viability of the project. They should be versed in how the national scene works, at least at an elementary level. They should know enough people at least to be able to talk to labels, booking agents, financiers. If they don't fulfil these requirements, they should hold a different role in your team, not that of manager.

- **Promoter:** At the start you only want to be filling local venues, or a couple of venues as best you can. A keen promoter can help with that. A good promoter is usually someone with great people skills, someone who knows the venues and the people who perform at those venues.

It helps if they have a decent understanding of recordkeeping and accounting, so they can pay (or keep track of payments from) relevant people such as the bands, the staff working the door, the venue, etc, when the time comes.

- **Social media person:** In the beginning this can be literally anyone with a camera who can follow you around at your gigs, etc, to capture the bits you can't by yourself and be able to post regularly in attractive ways. If they have experience with graphic design and so can create your artwork, that's even better.

What style of networking is best for you

Let's think back to the messages in Chapter Two. Your message might be like the first one:

> I don't give a fuck what I look like; I just go out in something comfy. I don't give a fuck about being a great guitarist or anything; I just like cool tunes and guitar bands. I don't give a fuck what people think. I eat bacon butties and I think life is about having loads of sex with fit people, drinking and having a boss time with your mates.

In this case, why are you going to networking events if you don't give a fuck?

Or your message might be more like the second one:

> I wouldn't be seen dead in a trench coat; I will only wear fabulous boutique clothing, and I love anything that sparkles. I think life is what you make it, and you gotta go after it and believe in yourself. I absolutely love Mimi Webb, Cardi B and Nikki Minaj. I tried the taster menu at Heston Blumenthal's Fat Duck restaurant last weekend. I was in long-term relationship, but it all broke apart, and now I'm just pushing on to get over it all.

If that's you, why are you going to *every* networking event, when really all you want to do is be seen in fabulous boutique clothing, and you love anything that sparkles? You should focus only on the networking events that fit your MO.

Good networking

Networking works best when it's totally seamless, and key to great networking are personality and memorability.

If someone turned up uninvited on your doorstep with a bunch of business cards and asking you to give them money, your immediate response would be to slam the door in their face. This is what most networking events are like – door-to-door salesmen, cold calling. That's why on the whole, they're mostly shit and accomplish little.

There's another approach, though. An event of *any* kind is always a good way to bring along someone you know, have a few drinks and have a great time. While you're there, there's no reason why you can't chat to someone new and tell them what you're up to.

Hoovering the room for business cards won't get you anywhere, and it's also seen as too needy. You're more likely to meet people when you're having a blast than when you're networking like a robot.

One of the main things that fails about networking events is that they're not targeted enough. Good networking comes down to getting to know the specific person who can assist you. For example, if I'm a musician who wants to play at your venue, I don't want to know who painted the room, who made the sandwiches and who the electrician was. I want to know who I need to speak to so I can perform in the venue. No further networking is required – I need to meet just that one person.

TRY THIS NOW: Kickstarting your networking

Think of a venue you'd like to play at or a specific person you need to speak to.

If you don't know exactly who or what, how could you find out?

To find out specifically who to speak to, you can simply go up to the reception desk at the venue and ask. Otherwise, you can research people online or find them on social channels like LinkedIn.

Do your research and start trying to find the person or the place you need to move closer to. Don't get in touch right off the bat. Instead, simply find out what you can, learn what you need to, and then think about a plan to start engaging with them. Do this by demonstrating the quality of your *work*, not by being verbose.

Meeting the right person

Meeting someone specific can be exciting, and it can be difficult. If you tried to meet the Pope, the chances are you'd be stonewalled! There's a specific way you should handle meeting that specific person, which I'll lay out for you here.

How to get in touch

Often big celebrities, CEOs and other people of importance look like they're in control of their ship. However, they often have little to no say at all in what their day-to-day schedule looks like. Organising their diary will likely be down to their tour manager, their manager, their agent or their personal assistant. If you want to support Taylor Swift on tour, say, it likely isn't Taylor you need to speak to. She will most definitely sign off on the decision, but most big stars are quite happy to let their employees do the scheduling for them because it's too much work for them as massive media personas.

If you're not aiming for Taylor Swift – if you're only interested in getting to know the promoter at your local pub, say – then a lot of these complications won't be in your way. All you need is to do your research, and here are three points to get you started:

1. **Internet.** Online searches are quick, free and easy and will give you a lot of information. Mostly people who pull strings *want* to be contacted, but they want to be contacted by someone serious who knows their business and understands them. Check out their social media, work profiles and websites to learn more about them. This can help you understand what they're interested in, which makes talking to them easier.

2. **Mutual contacts.** Ask anyone who works in the same circles as the person you want to meet for help. If you and the person you're trying to contact have mutual contacts, you can ask your friends to introduce you. They might have good things to say about you and help you connect.

3. **Common ground.** Before you reach out, think about what you have in common with that specific person. Do you like similar things, work in similar areas or know the same people? This can make your connection feel much more organic – a natural progression rather than a cold call.

When to get in touch

In general you should send emails between Tuesdays and Thursdays. If the email is to somebody on tour, timing depends on their schedule (which could be unbelievably busy).

If it's an email to a director or a person likely to be sat at a desk or busy in meetings, avoid Mondays. Monday mornings are awful for busy people. They might just have had a great weekend, perhaps with loads of travelling. They may be hungover or going through a divorce. Or maybe they simply can't be bothered full stop – who knows? However their weekend was, they've been torn away from their bed to get back in the office, dealing with a mountain of nonsense. The coffee machine has broken, the new intern doesn't have a clue, and there it is: your email sat in an avalanche of emails in an inbox full of imploring hopefuls trying to reach them from the previous Friday night. If you want your email to find a total stranger in a good state of mind, avoid Mondays!

Fridays are the same story but for different reasons – no one cares after a busy week. Everyone's thinking of one thing and one thing only: the weekend. Fridays are the catchup days, the last-minute emergencies. For the majority of people, this isn't the day to dedicate serious brain energy to inviting new requests or getting more asks.

Finally, under no circumstances should you initiate a cold call during the weekend. That's like firing the first shot in a duel, and the chances of success are slim. People already face a barrage of phone calls and emails throughout the week, and the last thing they appreciate is an intrusion into their privacy during the weekend, especially on Sundays. It is imperative that you refrain from sending new requests on weekends, even to individuals you know. I for one have an unshakeable rule that I do *not* answer any calls on weekends. The weekend is my time; weekdays are work time. Failing to observe the unwritten and sacred etiquette of the weekend will likely lead to an immediate cold fish.

While there are of course people who welcome and are open to business discussions on any day of the week, serious people shut down their calendars on weekends because they have their own personal lives to lead. The overarching message is simple: people lead busy lives. If you want someone to take you seriously, it's important to find out (if possible) about their schedule, and gauge their time appropriately and respectfully.

How to get in the friend zone

You think you're ready to contact them directly, but are you absolutely sure this person will welcome that? Some people don't like or are even offended by you contacting them directly, because they see it as yet another burden in an avalanche of people trying to get them to do something for them.

If you have the person's email or phone number, you could send them a nice message introducing yourself and explaining why you want to talk. Make sure you're clear about what you want right from the off instead of trying to seduce them in a longwinded plot. You should generally talk in a personal way; and make sure your message is hitting all the common ground features – you know someone, they introduced you, you both like cats, you've been a fan of their work – anything at all that levels the playing field.

Show that you've done some research about them and that you want to talk, but don't overcook it. A statement like *I see in 2008 you were awarded the best businessman award* is not something that someone on the move and battered with requests wants to hear. They know their own history.

Crucially, you have to think about what you can offer *them*. Maybe you have useful information, something that could help them or an idea for how they could benefit from the introduction too.

You want all of this to come across in as little information as possible. Absolutely nobody has any time anymore. I've seen people erupt in meetings because their phone has pinged and they see they're expected to read a short paragraph in their inbox.

What you can expect back

Don't expect any warm replies. It's most likely the person you're contacting will essentially say, *What the fuck do you want from me?*

These are five genuine responses to entire introductory emails I've had from people in senior positions.

- A thumbs-up emoji.
- 'No from me thnx.'
- 'Yes I can do that.'
- 'When do you need this by Ben?'
- A blank message, followed by 'Sent from my iPhone.'

In contrast, here are three genuine responses from people in my local venues:

- 'Yeah, sounds great. Do you have a website I can look at?'
- 'Hi Ben, lovely to meet you. Yes, I think we can do that here. What sort of night are you looking to put on, and how many people are you expecting?'
- 'We don't really do that here, Ben, but I know that [Amy] is looking for some acts to promote and would be interested in talking to you. I've put her on CC.'

You can see that the responses in the latter are still brief but that people at the local level have much more time for you. They are generally more willing to throw you a bone or at least an apology, an explanation or another potential avenue you can discuss.

Don't be deterred by curt responses from harder-to-reach people. This is just about knowing your industry and understanding that people with increased amounts of responsibility simply don't have spare time. That may be an indication that they are in fact not the right person to speak to, and that you should try speaking to someone lower in the ranks. In that case, repeat the process again with someone who's down a notch or two.

Whoever you're contacting, respect their time. Remember that they will be very busy and are likely juggling marital difficulties, family dramas, illnesses and a host of other things that you're not aware of. If they can't reply right away, don't worry. Be patient and understanding.

How to persevere

If you don't make the connection the first time, you may need to keep going to events where you think the other person will appear. If there's a networking event, workshop, conference or gig, say, with things you both like, try going. If they're there too, you can meet them in person and say something like, *I sent you an email a few weeks ago, but don't worry – I understand you're busy.* There is a fine balance here too, because you don't want to come across as a stalker.

Keep trying, nicely. If they don't reply at first, don't give up. Lots of people get inundated with messages. You can send a polite follow-up message after a grace period of a week or two to show you still want to talk. Just do not send anything the same week, otherwise you'll be seen as a needy weirdo.

Always remember, good connections are built on being nice and being yourself. Whether you're reaching out for work or simply to be friends, be honest and respectful. That's the best way to start a good relationship.

Get to the club and go see some bands. Get involved and be the person who created some things that are worth talking about. Building real relationships is key.

Key things to remember

A quick summary of the main points on how to meet someone specific:

1. Get in there.
2. Say what you want as concisely, directly and to the point as you can.
3. Say it nicely.

4. Get out of their way promptly.

5. Don't hassle them for a response. No response is still a response!

6. Keep persevering, trying new places and being careful not to overdo it.

If you finally get a small introduction, try to meet up in person. 99% of the deals I've ever done have taken place because something happened in person. You choosing whether or not to buy the other person a cup of coffee can often mean the difference between succeeding and failing.

How to choose your manager

No matter the strength of the team, management is often the difference between success and failure. Managers don't necessarily need to be from a particular institution, agency or label. They only have to be able to deliver, and to understand you and what you're trying to achieve. Bottom line: they should have the ability to leverage your art and open doors. If they can't do that, you're better off managing yourself and building your team. I've seen great managers who are simply determined business owners, savvy friends, connected family members and other incarnations.

A word of caution: on no account should a close member of your family be your manager. Experiences of well-known artists, from Britney Spears to Michael Jackson, clearly articulate the pitfalls. It's fine to have encouraging parents who are supportive, and some people even have parents that work in the music industry. It's tremendously difficult, though, for others to work with an overprotective 'Dadager' or 'Momager'. They will ultimately be too close to the project to maintain objectivity, and many industry teams actively avoid them. It's notoriously difficult to build teams around Dadagers and Momagers too, because nobody feels like they can say what needs to be said about their sons and daughters. It's quite difficult to look a parent directly in the eye and tell them with some ferocity that their child is shit at something!

Where and how to start

A great place to look for a manager is the Music Managers Forum (MMF – https://themmf.net). Details for the office secretaries or even personal details of some of the best managers in the world appear on there. Some of my personal favourite networking events for managers (and others) have been:

- Tile Yard events in London
- Music Managers Forum (MMF) networking events in London
- Sound City in Liverpool

- Manchester Music City
- NAMM in California
- CAAS in Nashville
- Music City Networking in Nashville
- Merita in Barcelona
- LANDR in Paris

If you are making cold calls to get in touch with managers, follow through with all of the networking steps I've outlined earlier in this chapter. That means that when you're getting in touch with them, you'll at least have an educated approach and something to deliver if they are interested.

Conduct research to find professionals who specialise in the areas you need help with. This can be done with any or all of the following:

- Look for credentials, experience, reviews and testimonials to assess managers' expertise and reputation.
- Seek recommendations from friends, family members or colleagues who have had positive experiences with professionals in the relevant fields.
- Try scheduling some initial consultations with potential professionals to discuss your needs

and see if you feel comfortable working with them. Use this opportunity to ask questions, understand their approach and evaluate their communication style.

Once you have identified a potentially ideal manager, you need to dig deeper. To do this:

- Make sure you talk clearly about what you want and what you expect.
- Share what you hope will happen, and work together to decide on realistic goals.

Different managers will want different things from you, depending on the kind of music you make. Managers are just as busy as artists, and they're always looking for new opportunities or a gap in the market where you can fit in. If an artist only expects to get money, guidance and recordings for free from their manager, things won't work out. You need to realise that you have to work hard and pay for most things in the beginning. Why? Because it's *your* career, not theirs!

Good managers will listen to you and give you useful advice as part of their role. They will generally take a standard fee of 20%, because they need to think smart, plan well, make deals and stay updated on what's happening in the market. That is a full-time commitment, with many headaches!

John Garrison: It's a people business

I first met John Garrison in 2011. We've been friends ever since, and we bump into each other once in a while when our schedules allow.

Now a renowned musician, John has accomplished many incredible achievements, including producing for the likes of Ed Sheeran, touring with James Blunt and founding the British alt-rock band Budapest.

When I had the opportunity to catch up with John online, while he was on tour in Germany with James Blunt, he shared some valuable insights gained from his experiences. He revealed that sometimes, 'you can want something too much. That was definitely the case for me when I was younger. I was desperate for a record deal.' When he finally got one, he explains, he realised it was only a small piece of the puzzle. Getting a song on the radio seemed like a huge achievement, but even that was just one part of the bigger picture.

He learned that success in the music industry requires a combination of factors. You can have an incredible song, but if you don't have the right support system or opportunities, it won't reach its full potential. 'You still need the element of luck,' he says.

However, John emphasises the importance of putting in the hours and hard work. He believes that when opportunities arise, you must be prepared to seize them. When the opportunity presents itself,

> It's not enough to say, 'OK, I'll start practising now!' Whether it's in songwriting, playing an instrument or singing, you have to be ready – preparation is key.
>
> In recent years John had an eye-opening experience during an audition with James Blunt. He discovered that it wasn't solely his bass playing skills that were important but also the way he conducted himself. John explained that James is a military man, and that respect and discipline are ingrained in him. It didn't matter how talented John was as a musician; what mattered was how he carried himself. It was the night out with James that sealed the deal: 'There is absolutely no space for egos... I learned fairly early just to leave the ego at the door... Everybody's on the same team.'
>
> John's journey highlights the importance of networking properly and showing humility to be part of a team.
>
> You can hear the full interview on my *More in the Moni* podcast at www.moreinthemoni.com.

Networking comes naturally to some people, while others may take a little longer to master it. It doesn't matter. The key is for it to become natural. When nothing is forced and relationships blossom naturally and organically only then can real work be achieved.

EIGHT
Make Plans

The broad strokes of a solid plan – between you and anyone else you work in close partnership with – in the music industry are outlined in the chapters of this book:

1. Know your history
2. Stay true to your message
3. Make music
4. Explore your craft
5. Perform live
6. Grow your community and scale it up
7. Get a team

8. Make plans

9. Be resilient

10. Craft your story

Keeping this fixed into your daily focus is difficult to do, which is exactly why you need to make plans and keep reviewing them.

First, you have to communicate your plans clearly. I can't count the teams I've seen totally collapse purely because they don't communicate properly. When you do finally find your guitarist, your promoter, your potential manager or whoever it is, it's imperative you are both crystal-clear about expectations and what the terms are at each step of the way. This chapter is about the value of making a clear plan and how to do it.

There is nothing seedy or unsavoury about saying what you will and won't work on, how long you're going to be working on it and for what fee. Without laying these terms out clearly at the beginning of every gig, songwriting session, campaign or action of any kind, you run the risk of destroying your team because of poor communication.

One reason teams collapse early on is because they started out as a group of friends, getting together to have some fun playing music in the pub. When, over time, that relationship evolves into a business arrangement, the team members don't have a proper understanding of their roles and responsibilities.

There's nothing wrong in saying to someone, *Will you do X for me? There's no money in it, but I need it by Friday.* Leave it open to people to decide whether they believe in you enough to devote their free time to you. If you can't rope them in, though, you might need to put some money on the table.

Money talks

You don't have to offer ridiculous fees for things you need, but you do need to know that paying someone for their time will get you far more respect and reliable work than when people do things for no payment.

When people aren't compensated for their work, they often feel they can take their time and work at their own pace. I've witnessed countless artists lose band members, collaborators or content creators because they failed to establish clear terms but still expected pictures or content to be completed by certain deadlines. If they'd paid for the work and the person didn't deliver, they would have every right to criticise that person's work ethic. When you don't pay people, though, it gives the impression that their work isn't valued enough to warrant compensation.

A short fictional story – Janet and Dave

Janet ran a small, bustling café on the corner of Elm and Vine. The café had charm, a loyal crowd, and pastries to die for, but Janet wanted more. That's when she thought of Dave. Dave was her old friend from college, a talented web developer who had helped many small businesses grow.

One evening over coffee, Janet asked if he'd help her revamp her online presence. 'It'll be good for your portfolio!' she added with a smile.

Dave agreed. They were friends, after all, and he wanted to see her succeed. Plus, he'd always felt he owed her for those years she'd been there for him in college. The first project – designing a new website – took a few weekends, but Dave didn't mind. He could handle it.

Janet's needs kept growing, though. She asked for tweaks, new features and eventually a full e-commerce store. 'I promise, when business picks up, I'll pay you back!' she assured him.

Dave, eager to help, kept saying yes.

Months passed, and Dave's other work began to slip as his time became more invested in Janet's promises. Freelance clients grew frustrated with his delays, and his once-thriving reputation started to tarnish. Late nights for Janet's café left him drained, and soon he was struggling even to make enough money for his rent. Each time Janet asked for help, though, she'd call him her saviour, her lifeline, and he couldn't say no.

> One day Dave glanced around his tiny, cluttered apartment and realised he hadn't updated his own website in months. Bills were piling up, his stress was rising, and he hadn't taken on a new client in ages.
>
> Finally, he asked Janet if she could pay him even a small fee. She looked surprised.
>
> 'Oh, Dave, I wish I could, but right now, every penny is tied up in the café.'
>
> The realisation hit him like a cold wave – his kindness had become her convenience. Janet's business was thriving while his own was crumbling.
>
> With a heavy heart, Dave finally set a boundary. He told her he'd help her one last time, but after that, she'd need to find someone else. Janet looked hurt, almost offended, but Dave knew he had no choice.
>
> In the months that followed, Dave slowly rebuilt his life. It was tough, but each small victory felt hard won and honest. While his friendship with Janet never quite returned to what it once was, he'd learned something valuable: a gift given freely can be as costly as any debt if it goes unpaid for too long.

Stating your terms

To avoid mess – like the miscommunications and assumptions people made above – always make sure you discuss your terms for collaborating with each other, and most important, how much it's all going to cost. You need to do this, no matter who you're working with and what they do. The whole point of contract law is to stop miscommunications and assumptions for this very reason.

You don't necessarily need a contract, but you do need to write your terms down somewhere. At the least, share a brief email or a text message, detailing exactly what you want. As long as you have some kind of reply from the people involved, saying they've seen and accept your terms, that is often all you need.

Key points for your terms

The following list gives a good initial framework for what your terms need to include:

1. **Brief.** Discuss what the work, the event or the project is, and outline genuinely what's involved.

   Example: *I want you to play in my band for an upcoming gig.*

2. **Expectations.** Manage everyone's expectations of what you want from the outcome.

   Example: *I want you to play in my band for an upcoming gig, and you will need to do rehearsals. I want the gig to go as smoothly as possible because it's for a potential support tour.*

3. **Timing.** Discuss when you need it completed by.

   Example: *I want four rehearsals, starting next Wednesday, 10am – 1pm every week, and you will need to bring your drums.*

4. **Payment.** Discuss what the fees will be, including details about timing.

   Example: *It will cost me £12 to book a rehearsal room each time, which I'll pay in full. I'll pay you £50 for your hard work after the gig is completed, but I will take all the money from ticket sales.*

Get some feedback on your plans and adapt

A good plan can be changed whenever needed, and you need to keep making changes to match what people want now. The digital world we're living in is always changing, which makes it vital to stay updated. Keep learning and see if what you're doing is working well. If not, adapt.

Management plans

A big thing to know about the way managers plan is that they will no longer go in front of your project, but they'll get behind what you're doing. That means that if you're not putting in effort or bringing something to the situation, there's nothing for the manager to manage.

Managers will support something that's already showing promise. This means you have to do all the things I've mentioned before and create a good package – having great songs, working hard, being determined, having a good team, a good presence on social media, and having good relationships, doing good live shows, and so on. Only then will a good manager think about working with you and planning ahead. This is because it's frankly too hard to drag an artist through, and it's too easy for an artist to quit once a manager has put all the work in.

Ultimately, I see seeking management as a collaborative effort. It's not a relationship where the artist works for the manager, or vice versa. A great management relationship is one where the artist and the manager are working in tandem with one another for the common goal. Each brings different skills to the table, but ultimately, great management relationships want to build an effective team. You are both essentially business partners in the same project.

Often in the beginning people look for managers for one reason alone: laziness. Artists often don't want to book gigs or understand how money works or pay for recordings, and they think that a manager will do all this for them. This is *not* the case. A manager is knee-deep in planning, even when they have a *great* artist who's hard at work. It's you who has to already be doing these things before a manager gets involved.

Getting your team aligned with your message

Once you've got your team together and you're laying out your terms and plans for working with each other, you need to make sure you're all acting with one voice. That message is key to the totality of how your team operates, from the way it looks down to its tactics.

Below are ten examples of 'branded' messages on album titles. The name of each album and the body of work on the album would not be what they are without the artist first understanding what their message is.

1. *Add, Subtract, Multiply, Divide, Equals* – Ed Sheeran
2. *Compton* – Dr Dre
3. *Tissues and Issues* – Charlotte Church
4. *Menace to Society* – The Killers
5. *Smoke + Mirrors* – Imagine Dragons
6. *Break Every Rule* – Tina Turner
7. *In My Room* – Jacob Collier
8. *If All I Was Was Black* – Mavis Staples
9. *Melodrama* – Lorde
10. *Hotel Diablo* – Machine Gun Kelly

Can you see how *Tissues and Issues* conjures a different meaning and appeal to say, *Compton*? Then the titles of Ed Sheeran's catalogue portray a personality that's almost machine-like. They suggest something almost like a grand plan.

In My Room, on the other hand, suggests something private or self-made. Jacob Collier has publicly talked about the recording process in his home studio and how he feels inspired and connected deeply with his family.

Can you see how *Break Every Rule* by Tina Turner suggests her documentation of a struggle and how she conquered it? *If All I Was Was Black* by Mavis Staples immediately captures her genuine struggles with that of apartheid. Meanwhile, *Menace To Society* by The Killers almost immediately captures the type of music you're going to hear.

Your identity is your product, and you need your team to be clear what they're working on. It could shape the very look of your artwork, visuals and sonics. It will influence how you dress at live gigs and the way your producer makes your music sound. Fans, critics, audience, family – everyone – will react to whatever you've put out there. What you say and do paints a vivid picture of who you are, whether that's a gig, a song, a picture, a review or an interview, and that's what people *want* to know. Your message is the cornerstone of your brand, and this is what the team has to go on.

Collaborating with PR

A great team member to work with is a PR (public relations) person. This means you're paying someone else to do the majority of the work for you on your advertising and socials. To reach more people and make your brand known, it's good to get advice from marketing companies and use smart ways to get noticed – that's PR.

The advantage here is that these experts usually know how to use special strategies to help you. The disadvantage is that PR people can be extremely costly, and disappointingly, they're often *not* experts! You'd be surprised how many so-called strategists out there basically do the same thing you'd be doing but charge a lot of money for their services. The first important thing to know, therefore, is when to do this.

Whether or not you need PR is ultimately up to you, and it all comes down to money. If you can afford a budget of £1k to £10k per month to hand everything over, then you should go for it. Most of us, however, need to find a tipping point where the work in building a good image and presence can be handed over to a small team, for them to maintain and grow that work from there.

The time that you need to start getting help with PR is when all of these points apply:

- You feel confident with your message
- You're starting to hit your stride with the socials
- You are making some moves on the live scene
- You feel you have a story to tell
- You have a day job (or a manager) to help pay for PR

It's important to thoroughly do your research if you're going to engage with PR. You need to ask yourself first what you're actually planning to get out of them. For example:

- Are you looking to get some good blog support?
- Are you looking to be visible on some of their playlists?
- Are you looking for an Instagram boost?

Tonnes of PR entities offer these kinds of things but ultimately don't deliver nearly as well as an artist who has a good team and has been through the development processes, like honing the message, creating great music, networking and so on.

The pros of PR

The great thing about PR (if they're good) is that they:

- Have already built consistent relationships with blogs, radio, pluggers and all kinds of other relevant people
- Can often team you up with famous people, other brands or groups that are like yours
- Assist in joining you with online groups and social media to talk to people who are similar to you

PR is important, but knowing *when* to use it is even more important if you're to mitigate costs and spend wisely. If you're a new artist and short on money, and if you just really don't like posting on social media, then you don't need PR. What you need is motivation and a kick up the ass to do things on your own or assemble your team. You simply have to take control on the internet, get people interested, do the work, share stuff and build connections, and do it without spending lots of money.

Keeping your head in the right place

If you go about this pattern authentically and consistently, it will work. It's as simple as that. There is only one pitfall you should be aware of when it's working: confusing success on socials with happiness.

The more successful you get, the more progress you'll see yourself making, and the more momentum you'll feel you have. This is such a great feeling, and it propels you to think of more ideas, more content and more products. You'll then reach a critical point where you're not doing much at all and your fans and followers simply like, share, comment and buy whatever you put in front of them. This, however, is also psychologically dangerous.

You can use the positive feeling you gain from success to motivate you onwards. Push yourself forward and spread your message, show yourself and allow yourself to feel that you're doing well and you're mastering the steps.

This is the important bit, though: *do not* get sucked into an idea that looks like this:

Happiness = followers on social media

If you allow yourself to slip into that state of mind, then you cannot avoid the inevitable repercussion:

No followers on social media = no happiness

This is the death of many artists' accounts on socials. All the time I meet people who have a continual love-hate relationship with social media and are constantly rebranding, deleting accounts, turning off comments, reopening accounts, and so on. That's because they feel that whatever response they're getting is a direct reflection of their personal status. The simple truth, though, is that isn't the case!

Social media serves two purposes:

1. Fostering genuine connections and maintaining friendships
2. Promoting and marketing interests

Some people confuse these definitions by using a business tool to masquerade as a personal connection hub. To be clear: *real* friends actively engage, support and empathise. They're there for you, and they will phone you and turn up at your house if you need them. Clients, fans and followers, on the other hand, are anonymous and passive until personal interaction somehow alters their status. Distinguishing between these two ideologies is crucial for staying healthy; one must determine the primary purpose of their social media usage.

Ed Sheeran highlighted in an interview that he utilises Instagram and other social media platforms primarily for promoting his songs rather than for posting selfies.[6] He contended that those sharing selfies are essentially pitching themselves, seeking some kind of validation, support or acknowledgment.

If you're trying to do all the things we've been talking about to promote your music and get your arms around the business, then the purpose of your accounts should be unmistakable to you: you're promoting your business, *not* making friends! That means you have to accept the inevitable: someone out there won't like your business and will say so. Immediately, you should disregard trolls, naysayers and negative comments, and learn to respond to them in a positive way that benefits your *business*, not you personally.

James Blunt is a perfect example of this. While we adore James Blunt's music, his hilarious comebacks on X demonstrate how you can artfully turn a troll into a trend. Whether delivering candid truths, responding brutally to fans or simply being the most amusing presence on X, James Blunt's account encompasses it all.

TRY THIS NOW: Turning negatives into positives

How can you turn your frustration into content? Can you make it funny?

The next time you get unfollowed or trolled, or when someone says something you don't like, or even if you don't think you're getting the likes you deserve in general, ask yourself if you can channel your inner James Blunt.

Can you make it interesting in some way? Share posts and ideas that don't sound bitter, instead capitalising on something ridiculous about the situation.

Check out the socials channels of people who you admire and see how they tackle it.

The key lies in recognising the difference between building authentic relationships and leveraging platforms as professional tools. True friendships are grounded in trust, reciprocity and genuine care, while business promotion is about visibility, branding and growth. When we blur these lines, we risk diluting the value of both. By setting clear intentions for how and why we use social media, we can safeguard our wellbeing, preserve meaningful connections, and ensure our professional efforts remain purposeful and effective.

NINE
Be Resilient

Developing a healthy mindset is crucial for success in any field, and resilience is the foundation of that mindset. Challenges will come your way – musical hurdles, career setbacks and the unpredictable ups and downs of life – and how you respond to them is what will determine whether you thrive or burn out.

Building a strong support system – a team who has your back 100% – is another vital element of resilience. Absolutely no one succeeds alone. Every successful person, in music or any other field, has had others help them along the way.

In today's world, technology can either be a tool that propels you forward or an obstacle that drains your energy. Social media, for example, often gets a bad rap for damaging real-life connections. It's important, though, to understand that social media itself isn't inherently bad. It's just a tool, much like a car or an espresso machine, that serves a specific purpose. It's up to you to define how you use it. If you expect social media to create deep, meaningful relationships, you'll likely be disappointed. If you understand its function and use it wisely to connect with your audience, share your work and build your brand, it can be a powerful asset.

Your message – the heart of what you do – should always remain consistent. If the journey feels tough, express that in your work. Write songs that reflect the struggles of making music or the challenges of staying authentic in a competitive industry. Authenticity is a powerful tool for building a loyal fanbase and standing out. The more genuine you are to your fans and to yourself, the more people will connect with you on a real, human level.

Rob Wheeler: A story of resilience

Rob Wheeler's journey in music is one of perseverance, self-discovery and transformation. Raised in a small town in the northwest of England by a single mother, Rob found solace in music during his childhood.

'My heroes sang about cowboys, desperados and drifters,' he says. 'I write about what I see, what I feel. At the end of the day, I think that's what great country music is all about: sharing your truth so that someone else feels a little less alone.'

With a cheap guitar and a love for artists like Hank Williams, Johnny Cash and The Beatles, Rob escaped the struggles of being the 'poor kid in a council house', dreaming of a life on the road just like his musical idols. But the journey was not without its trials.

In 2012, a medical diagnosis with no cure forced Rob to confront a painful new reality, leading him into depression, addiction and a breakdown.

'Resilience in the music industry is sadly an essential skill and mindset; you must learn to endure,' he reflects. 'Unlike musical ability, talent or even prodigious levels of genius, it is not about craft or creativity. It is about accepting that whatever you write or play, you will be critiqued, and quite often harshly.'

Yet, Rob chose to turn these challenges into a turning point. 'I sought help, learned to help myself and realised that life and music are gifts,' he says. 'So, I poured my heart into them instead of self-destructing.' His newfound resilience became a foundation for his music, allowing him to embrace his vulnerabilities and channel them into his art.

With a small inheritance from his grandfather, Rob recorded his debut album, which quickly garnered critical success. It led to a global publishing deal and caught the attention of Nashville's music scene.

'Experience teaches you that, ultimately, art is not a competition,' Rob explains. 'Your passion to create music must outweigh the negativity that can be thrown at you from all directions, even sometimes from within your safe space and from people you love and trust.'

His project *Leave Tomorrow*, recorded in Nashville with industry legends like Jeff Trott, Steve Dorff and Frank Liddell, exemplified this ethos. The album, which blends UK and American country influences, became a chart-topping success, landing at number one on the Country album charts.

Rob's story is a testament to the power of resilience. 'It's vital to remember that self-belief, self-worth and self-preservation will carry you a long way,' he says. 'Make your music for you, write about what you see, hear and believe in; sing from the depths of your soul. By doing this, when you do get hit by negativity, you can at least look in the mirror and know you were authentic to your vision.'

Through authenticity and unwavering dedication, Rob has not only overcome personal adversity, but has become a standout in both the UK and Nashville music scenes, showing that resilience is the ultimate key to enduring the highs and lows of life in music.

'To thine own self be true, always,' Rob concludes, embodying the message of self-truth that has carried him through every step of his journey.

You can hear more about Rob's journey on my *More in the Moni* podcast at www.moreinthemoni.com.

Resilience is about being flexible

One of the first things I often hear about being resilient is that you have to be motivated and disciplined if you want to get to where you want to go. I'm not so sure, though, that resilience and discipline are even connected at all. To me resilience is not about being tough or immune – it's about being flexible. Flexibility can only take place when you're creative, when you're genuinely willing to improvise possibilities.

There are all kinds of motivational speaking memes and video clips of musicians, boxers, actors – inspirational speeches from people like Arnold Schwarzenegger, Jordan Belfort, Jordan Peterson, and so on – saying how they devoted their willpower to getting where they want to go. You've seen them, right? They're hugely inspiring. The clips themselves have stirring musical scores by Hans Zimmer, zingy angles and dramatic lighting. They make the speakers look like superheroes, progressing against all the odds. It's not surprising at all that we are inspired to teach our children to follow in their footsteps.

All of those people maintain that discipline is the magic ingredient that keeps you motivated and immune to setbacks and hard times. What I've seen in the music business, though, is that there comes a point where disciplining yourself to chase the dream sets off a chain reaction that for many has no return point and no payoff, and this only gets worse.

The fact is there are many celebrities and millionaires who have chased fame for centuries and are still not satisfied. Seeing their success, you'd think they were like a master race of beings, immune to stress or aberrant behaviour. As we know, though, the headlines are littered with the latest celebrity meltdowns, scandals and stories of billionaire predators, all describing people who are miserable or in jail because whatever their lives have become is still not enough for them.

The unending drive to move forward is caused early on by the influences of schools, celebrities and trends, and I feel it's a highly toxic game to play. On the whole, it's also not a successful one.

TRY THIS NOW: Nurturing resilience

Create a daily journal with the goal of nurturing resilience in your everyday life through getting your ideas down on paper. Think about the following questions and make notes:

- What are your core goals in music?
- Do those goals align with an overall life plan for yourself? Settling down? Travel? Money?
- Are any of those goals hurting more than they are helping? How?

You need to learn to say no

I recently watched the documentary about Avicii, which reminded me of all the music experiences I had in my teens.[7] I realised there was a real correlation between overall health and how exhausted I was from all the demands placed on me at the time.

I remember, as a teenager, knowing nothing about networking properly, building teams or managing my energy. All I understood was 'the goal', and I would do whatever it took to get there. This led to all kinds of wonderful things like discipline, project development, conquering personal challenges, focus, and so on, but the byproduct was often burnout.

I'm not sure if it's thanks to the wisdom of age or maturity, or both, but I'm now able to say no. As a father, a husband, a business owner and someone who has reached a different stage in life, I realise I wouldn't dream of taking on half the things I dealt with as a teenager. If someone criticised me now for not tweeting enough or selling enough tickets, I'd laugh in their face and tell them where to go.

That's just it, though – when you're younger or less mature, you feel the weight of the world on your shoulders, the need to impress or please people. When someone tells you that you can't stop a tour or give up for this or that reason, without the bulwark of life experience, you're often complicit in simply doing what people say, whenever they want it. This means you're busy chasing your own tail, often at the expense of your finances and your health.

This perfect storm, of the desire to reach a goal and the need to please, undoubtedly allows room for predators, opportunists and manipulative individuals – all kinds of low levels of life – to gain a foothold in a person's psyche and wreak havoc.

It made me sad watching the events in the Avicii documentary, as I'm sure it did everyone involved, including his family. I wonder if perhaps he could've said no to a few more things and given himself some headspace.

You need to learn to say no to things. It does you and your team the world of good to step back and build leisure time into your diary. Nobody is making you be in the music industry – you have every opportunity and right to drop everything you're doing right now and go and be a waiter in a restaurant. If you need a year off, take it. If you need more money, say so. If you have family commitments on a rehearsal date, rearrange the rehearsal.

You really can simply say no to people and lay out your terms. As long as you're clear with everyone on expectations, then it's perfectly feasible to evolve those expectations as the pressure increases.

Otherwise, what are you doing it for? Do you need to be famous or write music so badly that you're willing to die for it?

Discipline creates tunnel vision

Prolonged concentration takes effort, but unending concentration leads to collapse. If you have a goal and you want to get there, it's fine to apply yourself in a particular direction, providing you're open enough to divert that direction if it becomes necessary. I see students crying in corridors because they're not famous yet. They suffer enormous trauma from all the 'discipline is what it takes' talk because, like looking down a tunnel, concentration is the means to exclude all other thoughts in favour of one particular pattern of behaviour. The very word *concentrate* means to bring to the centre – *con* (with), *centrate* (centre).

Bringing a career goal or the need to be famous or recognised to the centre of your focus by its very definition shuts out anything else – your family, your creativity, your intelligence, your sense of peace or stability. Discipline of any kind brings suppression. To be disciplined in one thing, you have to suppress other things, and this takes tremendous effort. If you're a devoted zealot looking for an album deal, you're probably taking great pains not to be aware of anything else that might be just as good, just as useful or maybe even more fun or more fulfilling.

You see, discipline doesn't remove obstacles – it actually creates them. In music if you want to get good at the drums, you have to enquire, you have to practise, you have to be repetitive. However, you also have to share, to socialise, to have fun, to see what happens, to experiment.

Discipline works in certain situations and with specific agendas. It's not surprising the army prizes discipline, because the army wants things done in specific ways, with clear consequences if they're not done correctly. This doesn't mean, though, that treating your music career or your life like a military tour in 2001 Afghanistan is any way to be recommended or emulated.

'Becoming'

Often, officially successful people – like Michael Jackson, Avicii and many others – attest to the problem of having to constantly 'reach' for more. Those people might have effectively conquered the world – they don't need to work, they can go on lots of holidays and they have enough money to buy islands – but they haven't felt psychologically improved for all of that. If anything, successful people often feel the opposite. They never feel like they've 'arrived'.

To be resilient to all the obvious problems you'll encounter in the music business, you need the flexibility to be able to see the reality and irrationality of your own predicament – you want to become what you already are!

Whenever you say this is good but that is bad, it creates duality. Duality in our minds creates a battle. If you're striving for other things, you're living in a state of permanent duality. You're here now, but you want to be over there. This constant wrestling causes massive problems for people in all kinds of career situations. It's the thing that leads to the creation of the internet, the Empire State Building, Beethoven's *Fifth Symphony*; but it also creates competitiveness, expectation, anxiety, conflict, and in many cases depression and suicide.

We have a human need to 'become' something but don't realise that psychologically we more or less stay the same throughout our lives. Ask any person who is over fifty years old how they feel, and they will mostly say they feel more or less the same as they did when they were twenty, if a little creakier in places.

No matter what we perceive failure to be – whether it's not performing our best in a local pub or failing to sell out Wembley Stadium – defeat is extremely painful. The fear of failure seems to be directly proportional to the love of the goal, and this is why the gap – or the *battle* – gets set up in our minds in the first place. Put simply, it means we think the following: *I want to aim high, but aiming high also means I may have far to fall.*

Reaching is inevitable if we want to grow. As musicians, we all hope that our art will succeed. That takes effort, determination and a clear plan. But it's worth remembering that the desire to become something other than we are can be a source of inner conflict. Reaching always carries the risk of failure, and that's part of the process. Perspective is key: keep your motivation rooted in the music itself. Let the business side serve the art, not the other way round.

The rainbow effect

There's one final reason why discipline doesn't work as a strategy for being resilient in the changing music industry. It's because of something I've called *the rainbow effect*. It works like this: what if on one rainy Tuesday afternoon, the Lord God himself came by your house to tell you in person all the secret mysteries of the universe, but you missed him because you were out looking for him. Wouldn't that be the most tragic, maddening irony ever?

The lesson is this: when you're out of the house, you miss whatever chooses to stop by. We mentally 'leave the house' all the time when we discipline ourselves, and it's in our wandering that we get lost and are regularly not at home to receive something potentially life-changing.

The goal is like a rainbow. Discipline is the walk towards it. Yet discipline, on its own, never seems to be enough to allow you to reach the goal – much like chasing a rainbow will never bring you closer to it. This applies whatever field you're working in: whether it's the army, an orchestra or a corporate office. That's because no matter what success looks like to you, it requires more than just discipline alone. I believe it depends just as much on stepping back, observing and spending time with friends and family as it does on being proactive, determined and hard working. It's all about finding the right balance.

Have you ever noticed that it's impossible to deal with negative thoughts by having positive ones? In fact, trying to have positive thoughts can be the worst thing to do, because you'll be caught in the rainbow effect – thinking positively will only remind you that the reason you're thinking positively is because you're feeling negative! If life is kicking you in the nuts, 'thinking positively' about that will begin to do some strange things to your state of mind, because the very impulse to move towards a positive mood denies it from happening.

This happens to songwriters all the time. You can keep sifting through ideas for hours without coming up with anything. Then one morning you wake up, and for seemingly no reason at all, the ideas dawn on you and you can finish a song in minutes. The best songwriters are those who can tap into this energy. Instead of chasing ideas in the street, those people stop and allow the ideas to stop by the house.

This has been called the *negative principle* by Karl Popper.[8] Alan Watts called it the *backwards law*.[9] Meanwhile, it's what *mushin* in Japanese and *wuxin* in Chinese (written '無心', meaning *no mind*) refer to, in particular with Zen or Daoist ideas.[10] Here I'm calling it the rainbow effect for the simple reason that a rainbow is an illusion, and the closer you move toward that illusion, the more it vanishes.

This same effect happens everywhere in our lives. Here are some examples:

- If you ask someone out in a bar and are too keen and clingy, the first thing they do is try to get away from you. Conversely, the less you chase after someone, the more interested they become.

- The more you strive to be happy and loved, the lonelier and more afraid you become. On the other hand, the more comfortable you are in your own skin and the less you go looking for happiness, the more easily it finds you and the less afraid you are of losing it.

- The harder you work to micromanage a team, the more they loathe you; but the more you delegate to them and let them find solutions on their own, the more you're perceived as a great leader.

- The more you focus on keeping up with the Spotify algorithm, the more you feel like you're in a meat grinder. The more you focus on great music, done well with a great plan, the more the Spotify streams start happening anyway.

The aspiration to 'reach a destination' in the industry must always take a backseat. You need to be constantly aware of broadening your focus and your agendas, thereby embracing a wider perspective.

TRY THIS NOW: Aligning your goals

Make notes on all the following:

- Which goals are you focusing intensely on?
- Who are the people or opportunities that recently came your way that were *not* connected to your goal?
- Was there any opportunity you might've missed because you chose to ignore it?

Handling rejection

It's vital to learn how to handle rejection, especially since it happens a lot. Instead of letting rejection divide us or create more competition, we can use it to improve our business or technical understanding.

Mike Nelson: Embracing what comes

Mike Nelson, better known by his stage name Banners, is a celebrated musician from England, whose songs have graced the soundtracks of some of the most popular TV shows of the last decade.

Mike's musical journey began long before the world knew his name. Growing up in Liverpool, he sang in a special choir at a grand church, performing in venues across Europe. It wasn't until he moved to Toronto in 2015, though, that his career truly began to take shape. It was there that he released his first song, 'Ghosts', under the name 'Raines' – a track that eventually found its way into popular TV shows like *Suits* and *Teen Wolf*. Little did Mike know then, this was the start of something much bigger.

In 2018 Mike appeared on *American Idol*, showcasing his voice and gaining national attention. The following year he released his debut album, *Where the Shadow Ends*, marking a major milestone in his career. His songs continued to be featured in TV shows like *The Royals* and *Lucifer*; and in *Grey's Anatomy*, with 'Someone to You' playing a key role in an unforgettable episode involving Derek Shepherd's return.

In a candid conversation I had with Mike, he opened up about the unpredictable nature of his rise to fame.

He explained that he counts his fame professionally from the point he signed a record deal, around 2016, and that he's simply glad to have made it this far. When he thinks back to how much he didn't know back then, he says it's almost like he was thrown into a washing machine like a bunch of socks: 'There's loads of them, and you just get tumbled around, and then somehow... everyone else has gotten lost in there; it's just that you got your moment of luck.'

Mike wasn't shy about admitting that luck and uncertainty played a huge role in his journey, but he wasn't implying that it was only a matter of chance – far from it. He explained that you need luck, but you only get that luck if you work really hard. Even when you work your hardest, that one moment of luck can change everything. Sometimes the difference between your song making it onto a TV show or not is purely about that one person hearing it and sharing it with someone else.

It's easy to think of luck as some external force – something that happens by chance. Mike's story shows us that luck isn't purely random, though. It's a result of relentless effort, a willingness to embrace uncertainty, and the openness to take advantage of every opportunity that comes your way. It's about doing the work, staying humble and staying open to the unexpected. As Mike put it, you have to be nice to people and work as hard as you can, and then just be lucky.

Resilience doesn't mean fighting against life's twists and turns. It means embracing them. It's about being ready for the unknown, being flexible enough to ride the waves of unpredictability and trusting that even the most unexpected moments can lead to something extraordinary.

Today Mike continues to share his music with the world, including building a loyal fan base with over 550,000 YouTube subscribers and more than 328 million views. His story is proof that success isn't always linear, and that sometimes the best things happen when you embrace what comes your way.

You can hear more about Mike's journey on my *More in the Moni* podcast at www.moreinthemoni.com.

Diversifying your income

Financial resilience is as important as mental resilience, especially for musicians. Like many creative fields, the music industry is unpredictable. Whether you're just starting out or riding a wave of success, one thing is certain: diversifying your income can help you stay afloat during tough times and provide the stability you need to keep creating.

Relying solely on one income stream, whether it's from music sales, live performances or another single source, can be a risky way to build your future. Managing your finances carefully is one of the best ways to stay resilient, especially as your career gains momentum.

Let's face it: when you're young and just starting out, life can feel like a party – couch surfing, low-cost beers and living for the next gig or jam session. You might feel like you don't need to worry about saving money or diversifying your income, but the costs of living – from rent and groceries to transportation and new gear – are constant. As your responsibilities increase, your financial savvy also needs to evolve.

Consider these alternatives that can help ensure you're not relying on only one source of revenue:

- **Live performances and merchandise sales:** Touring and selling merch at gigs can be a huge revenue stream, especially when you're starting to build a fanbase. Even small shows can turn into profitable ventures.

- **Music teaching or coaching:** Whether through private lessons or group workshops, teaching can be a reliable and fulfilling way to make money.

- **Online presence:** Building a strong presence on platforms like YouTube or Patreon, or even on streaming services, can supplement your income. For many musicians today online content and engagement are essential components of their overall earnings.

- **Additional income.** Every bit counts, from part-time work in a bar to freelance music work, or creating a secondary source of passive income through your online presence.

The more you diversify, the better equipped you'll be to weather financial problems.

The power of financial health

Thinking about the future might not always feel exciting, but it's crucial. The more wisely you manage your money today, the more options you'll have tomorrow. For example, setting aside a small amount of money each week can add up to something significant over time. Even if you start with only £1 per week, £52 by the end of the year isn't a fortune, but it's a start. If you increase that to £10 a week, you'll of course have £520 by year's end. Imagine if you could scale that up even further, say £100 a week, saving £5,200 over the year.

Buying a home or securing your retirement might seem distant now, but developing the mentality of saving and planning will set you up for long-term success. It will allow you to make decisions from a place of confidence, not desperation.

Your time and energy are just as valuable as your money. Think about it: there are 168 hours in a week. If you're working 15 hours a week in a part-time job, you might be earning enough to cover your bills. That still leaves you, though, with 153 hours to dedicate to your passions: your music, your creativity, your dreams.

You could use the income from a part-time job outside of music to fund recording sessions, purchase new equipment or even invest in a professional music video. You can also explore other creative ventures like starting a YouTube channel or a podcast, or engaging in a live-streaming event. The more you think about your time as a resource, the more opportunities you create for yourself.

The 2020 global pandemic was a clear reminder of how even the most stable industries can be upended overnight. When the music industry came to a halt, many musicians found themselves scrambling to make ends meet. Those who had already diversified their income, though, had a cushion to fall back on.

When you manage your finances wisely, create multiple income streams and plan for your future, you're setting yourself up for success in ways that aren't immediately visible. They'll be the quiet factors, though, that keep your team in operation and allow you to sustain what you're doing until the bigger deals and opportunities start landing.

I always ask my own clients at the beginning to triple-check that they can afford me before they commit to us working together. If you're financially stable, with a job, gigs, royalties or other financial backup, it means you can invest in services like mine, in marketing, in a new guitar or in whatever else you want, without the threat of your rent not being paid or your parents being on your back.

MAKE MUSIC YOUR BUSINESS

TRY THIS NOW: Every bit counts

If you're new to saving money, start setting aside a small amount regularly. Whether that's £20 a week or £50 a month, the key is consistency.

Automate transfers to a separate savings account to make it a habit. Over time, as your financial situation improves, increase your savings.

Starting small and staying consistent will build your savings muscle without overwhelming your budget.

Good luck!

James Scroggs MBE: Roll the peanut

James Scroggs's career is a testament to the quiet power of small, consistent actions. It's not just his professional success that makes him remarkable, though; that also comes through his humility, his grounded nature and the way he approaches life. To know James is to understand how one small moment can snowball into something extraordinary; how even the most modest steps, taken with intention, can lead to profound accomplishments.

James has led major campaigns for brands like Mars and Budweiser, earning recognition for his creative approach. As account director for Stella Artois at Lowe Howard-Spink, he shaped the 'Reassuringly expensive' and Stella Bottle campaigns, making Stella the UK's most valuable beer brand.

By 2002, as VP of marketing at MTV Networks UK and Ireland, he strengthened MTV's global presence, launched hit shows like *Pimp My Ride*, and orchestrated the brand's twenty-fifth anniversary celebration. His career highlights also include the relaunch of ONdigital as ITV Digital, where the iconic 'Al & Monkey' campaign took off. Later, at SpinVox, he drove key partnerships and helped revolutionise voicemail-to-text technology.

James served on the board of several charitable organisations, including CALM (Campaign Against Living Miserably), which works to raise awareness of male suicide. He also supported the Institute of Contemporary Arts and Robin Wight's Ideas Foundation, focusing on using creativity to change lives. Perhaps the greatest lesson James taught me, though, wasn't about marketing or business strategies. It was about the art of momentum; the importance of embracing the detours of life; and how small, seemingly insignificant steps can lead to huge transformations.

James shared a wonderful piece of wisdom with me, explaining that success, in a sense, is a pathway laid out by someone else to tell us what the destination should be. He maintains, though, that in truth it's almost the opposite: to be truly yourself, you have to take a series of baby steps. Every day can be a baby step. If you chunk your world down, these small steps may seem childish in the grand scheme of things, but over time they accumulate into something bigger – something profound.

He used the metaphor of rolling a peanut across a table, explaining that if you roll a peanut or a rugby ball, it won't travel in a straight line. It will flip-flop, take detours, and bounce off the sides. The same applies to life, growth and careers. Unless you're prepared to accept that your journey won't always be linear, that you'll take some strange lefts and rights along the way, you'll be endlessly disappointed. You'll always feel like you've failed.

That's the secret to James's success. It didn't come from one big moment, one giant leap. It was the accumulation of countless small, deliberate steps. It was rolling the peanut, letting it take its unpredictable path and trusting that it would get where it needed to go, even if it took some unexpected detours.

James's journey is a reminder: Small actions, small decisions and small moments can snowball into something extraordinary. The key is to keep moving forward, one step at a time, and to trust that each little achievement, each small detour, is part of a much bigger picture.

Just like the peanut rolling across the table, your path may not be a straight line, but as long as you're moving, you're progressing. One small step today might lead to the next big breakthrough tomorrow.

Roll your peanut, and see where it takes you.

> For more insights from James, listen to the full interview on my *More in the Moni* podcast at www.moreinthemoni.com.
>
> *Note: If you or someone you know needs mental health support, there are people and organisations who can help. Two of those can be found at www.themix.org.uk and www.thecalmzone.net.*

The importance of being happy and healthy can't be overstated, but just as crucial is the ability to be flexible, to step back and to let whatever comes your way shape your mindset and your work just as much as discipline and determination. Maintaining a healthy balance is key: do what you love, use your mind to change what's within your control, but also leave space for the unexpected to unfold. This only happens when you're able to relax and let go of trying to control everything.

TEN
Craft Your Story

To truly break into the industry, it's crucial to weave a compelling narrative and craft a story. This chapter talks about the power of a compelling and authentic narrative and how you can create one.

The direction of your story

To get anywhere in the music industry, you have to tell a story that's public, visible and can be relayed in a single paragraph to 'industry people'. The same applies whether you play in a wedding band or a tribute act, if you're working on a cruise ship or you're a signed artist with a deal.

A story encompasses various elements:

- Your social media metrics
- The number and locations of gigs you've performed
- Details about your songs – their influences, recording locations and production or publishing credits
- Your background, age and any noteworthy endeavours you're involved in, eg building a strong following at a specific venue, organising charity gigs or collaborating with a celebrity

All of these aspects grab the attention of industry professionals and fans alike.

A well-crafted story is essentially an industry-facing idea, but it also simultaneously gives your fans and audience something to relate to – a way for them to connect with a rising star, a movement, a feeling of momentum. It helps them understand who you are and where you come from, and also what you've done and where you're going next.

Stories are memorable, and they help industry people and fans alike to get a measure of your 'worth' and your likeability. What sucks about this is that people will gather around and support the artist that has a better story but not necessarily the artist who makes better music. That just means you need to create a great story, though.

When people remember your story, they are more likely to remember you as an artist and give you the coveted follows on social media. A great story nearly always leads to increased recognition and a stronger fan base, which sets you apart from the crowd in a competitive industry. It helps you stand out and be more noticeable among the sea of artists.

The message vs the story

A story is different from a message. While your message focuses on your values, your beliefs and the meanings behind your music for your fans, your story describes your journey within and for the industry.

If you recall the section on crafting your message, I gave three examples. Let's look here at the third one:

> I'm shy, and I worry what people think of me. I tend to try to avoid being around lots of people. I suffer from bad anxiety and find it difficult to talk to people. I just wear stuff I think is cute, and I'm not too bothered about what I look like. I'm really into The Cranberries and Fleetwood Mac, and I enjoy

hanging out with my friends in my house. I'm gay, and I sometimes feel isolated from my family, but my boyfriend has been a rock through all the hard times.

This is a message, but it's *not* a story – your story is what you *do* with your message. This is an important distinction. Some of the information here will contribute to your story, but some of it is entirely irrelevant in terms of making moves on the scene.

Here are some other important points about your story:

- It is what others will say about you.
- It's the image that people see.
- It's what people report back to their bosses.
- It's what fans read in the magazines and the blogs.
- It's what A&R people ask at every pitch meeting.
- It is about how your message is faring with the world.

Your story can be conveyed as a blog entry, a press article, an EPK (electronic press kit) or biography, or in a casual conversation to a tastemaker. Whoever you're talking to, the story has to be the same.

Here's an example of a strong story:

Discover the electrifying rise of Person X, a self-taught singer-songwriter and producer who's been captivating audiences for three years with her raw talent and original sound. From iconic venues like The Bedford in Balham, The Half Moon in Putney and The Cavern in Liverpool, to a viral TikTok moment and a sold-out show at the O2 Ritz in Manchester, Person X is making waves. Her unique sound blends the soulful depth of Angie Stone with the raw, lyrical edge of Azealia Banks, creating an unforgettable musical experience. If that isn't enough, catch her surprise busking session with Stormzy in Las Ramblas! Praised by DIY magazine as 'a force to be reckoned with', Person X is on the rise. Watch this space – she's just getting started.

Here's an example of a poor one:

Person Y has written four or five good songs but hasn't released them. He is waiting to build his following and is only just getting onto the live scene. His following is around five to ten fans per gig in his hometown, but his teachers in his university think he's really got amazing potential, since he repeatedly showed this in his school performances. His friends say, 'Out of everyone in our year, he's easily the best songwriter we know.'

I'm sure the reasons that Person X's story is better than Person Y's are self-evident, but let's comb through them nonetheless, starting with comparing their achievements and experience:

- Discover the electrifying rise of Person X, a self-taught singer-songwriter and producer who's been captivating audiences for three years with her raw talent and original sound. From iconic venues like The Bedford in Balham, The Half Moon in Putney, and The Cavern in Liverpool, to a viral TikTok moment and a sold-out show at the O2 Ritz in Manchester, Person X is making waves.
- Person Y has written four or five good songs but hasn't released them.

Straight away you can see Person X has far more story to tell. It shows she's been writing more, performing non-stop and so is probably used to touring to some extent. It names actual, credible venues, whereas Person Y's statement is only full of hearsay and vagaries. Person X's opening statement shows she is hungry, driven and has some understanding of the business. Person Y doesn't have any business – he's only got four songs! Person X's statement also implies that she probably knows people and has some fans, otherwise how would she be getting the gigs and making them financially supportive?

The stories also include the following statements:

- Person X, [is] a self-taught singer-songwriter and producer...
- Person Y is waiting to build his following and is only just getting onto the live scene.

Implied in Person X's statement is that she writes, records and performs everything, which shows a lot of skill, dedication and hard work in itself. This statement is also qualified by the next sentence in her story, her prodigious live activity showing that she must have an arsenal of songs. Person Y, by comparison, has absolutely nothing going on. If he's 'waiting' to build his following, he's delusional. Person X isn't waiting – she's *doing* it!

Naturally, we could dissect the rest of both statements all day long, but I'm sure you get the picture. You'll see essences of each artist's message in their story, but it's the story itself that excites people and calls them to action. Gatekeepers of all shapes and sizes can't do much without a story, which means it's up to the artist to craft theirs with as much impact as possible. They also then need to make the real-world moves to keep building their story.

The tenets of storytelling in music

Here are eight crucial points to help you craft a first-class story:

1. Background

2. Angle

3. Headline

4. Quotes

5. Structure

6. Achievements

7. Prospects

8. Presence

1. Background

Start by thoroughly researching and writing out your background, your genre, your influences and your recent accomplishments. Review your message as well as what you have achieved with it. Understand what your music style is, what your lyrical themes predominantly cover, and take note of any noteworthy performances you have done.

2. Angle

Determine your unique angle or cornerstone for your story to wrap around. This could be a recent album release, a successful tour, a personal journey or an innovative approach to music. The angle should be intriguing and relevant to listeners and readers of all ages, types and positions.

3. Headline

Develop a headline that captures the attention and the essence of your angle. A strong headline entices readers to delve in and sets the tone for what to expect. An angle such as *This will blow your f%$king head off!* is way more enticing than *Has done three gigs*.

4. Quotes

Write down or try to get some interviews with genuine press outlets or blogs to gather insights, anecdotes and quotes that genuinely exist in the web or in print. Bloggers at websites like www.submithub.com and www.musosoup.com will review your music and give you some honest, quotable feedback and a Google presence. As you rise the ladder, you're able to get the bigger publications to talk about you.

5. Structure

Organise your article or story into a coherent structure. In case an A&R person asks your manager what you're up to, get your manager to rehearse what they're going to say. Incorporate high-quality images in your story, and have them preloaded somewhere accessible so that if anyone asks your manager in a meeting what you look like, the images will be easy to find. The obvious place to put these (and where most people go first) is an attractive social media platform like Instagram. You could experiment with promotional photos, album covers and concert shots.

6. Achievements

Make a list and highlight what you've achieved so far. As you're starting out, this can be absolutely anything. If you haven't done much, it could be a sign you should be doing more. You can always upsell the things you're doing if you need to in the early days, making them sound as impressive as possible, for example talking about chart-topping songs, collaborations with renowned artists, awards and recognition of any kind.

7. Prospects

Weave a narrative throughout your pitch to create a sense of progression. People want to know not only where you've been but also where you're going next. You're trying to sell to them whether they should hire you, sign you and follow you, and they'll want to know where you're heading. Share some anecdotes that provide a glimpse into your journey, describing not just your triumphs but also some things you've struggled with. That will add authenticity to your story, plus people will know you've learned and gained experience.

8. Presence

Depending on the platform, consider embedding music samples or links in your music or videos. Share your story on every single platform you have, and shout about it from the high hills. Add to it over time, and keep evolving the message as you grow your vision. Promote your story across social media, your website and relevant music forums – wherever it's appropriate. Let people know you're out there! Engage with any comments, feedback and critique you get to foster a sense of community.

Next are some questions to help you think along the right lines. Make notes now, then keep coming back to those notes to see what's changed or you can improve what you've written:

- What is your story? Where did you come from?
- Who are your influences?

- What are your recent (preferably musical) accomplishments?
- What are you trying to say? What is your message?
- Is there anyone notable or famous in your team?
- How many live shows have you done, where were they and did they sell out?
- What live events/releases or opportunities are happening within the next six months?

Don't just chase the money!

Trying to develop a powerful story is infinitely more valuable than merely chasing labels or finances. Don't just chase the money. Once you get caught up in trying to make it, all kinds of strange things start happening to you, as outlined below.

Concentrate on the story you're putting out into the world and what you can do to make it materialise in interesting ways. Once the story is present and the team can make it materialise, the money will follow. Focusing on the message you share with the world and how it comes to life is paramount. Even though money matters, there are two good reasons for putting your story first:

1. Authenticity
2. Headway

1. Authenticity

When you focus on your story, it helps you stay true to what you believe in. If you chase money instead, you might do things that don't genuinely match who you are. A strong story can stick around for a long time, even when money comes and goes.

If you genuinely care about your story, it can keep you motivated and excited. More importantly, it can keep you in business. Money alone might not give you the same kind of satisfaction or inspiration, but money alone is boring; and on the whole, people distrust people with bottomless pockets trying to be famous. When people see you're serious about your story, they trust and respect you.

2. Headway

Focusing on your story often leads to creative and smart ideas. You'll find cool ways to get your story out there, which over time will also gain you attention and financial support.

Amelia Dimoldenberg, the creator and host of the web series *Chicken Shop Date*, had the genius idea of interviewing celebrities at fried chicken restaurants, often using her sarcastic, deadpan and awkward humour to create unique and hilarious moments. Once the idea caught fire on the internet, the show began to get recognition, then funding, then sponsorship, and it all carried on to a success story from there. When you're dedicated to your story, it gives you things to discuss and something for people to share and talk about too.

Remember, it's possible to make money by sharing your story, but when you care more about money than the message itself, you might make choices that hurt the power and meaning of what you're saying.

> **Burrito Baby: The cost of chasing the quick buck**
>
> The pitch was simple: 'Let's write a song called "Burrito Baby" – something like "Crazy Frog" or "Gangnam Style". This could be huge!'
>
> At first I laughed, but the enthusiasm behind the plan got me wondering: *Could this actually work?* Before long, I was on board.
>
> A producer friend and I sketched out the track in ten minutes, but it felt flat. Hoping to salvage it, we brought in a seasoned (and now very expensive) mix engineer who thought we'd lost our minds but agreed to help anyway.
>
> Next, we needed a voice. A session singer gamely delivered the chorus, belting out 'All I want is burritos!' while laughing through every take. A promoter suggested that to add more colour we should include a quirky spoken line from a European student. I remembered someone I'd met at a

conference and offered her a small fee to record it. Sitting in her flat in Sheffield, listening to her pronounce *bear-it-oh*, I couldn't help but ask myself, *What am I doing with my life?*

Still, we pushed on – mixing, refining, designing logos, even launching a website. I'd poured nearly £700 into travel, recording and promotion. This was going to be big, right? Well... no. When it came down to it, everyone assumed somebody else had the industry contacts – and nobody did. The track landed with a thud. Potential collaborators recoiled, and the whole thing fizzled out to nothing.

Three months of effort and a French-accented *bear-it-oh* later, all I had was a bunch of questions and a chaotic pop experiment sitting on my hard drive, for no reason at all. At first, it felt like a disaster. But with time, I've learned to laugh at the absurdity of it all. 'Burrito Baby' has become less a failure and more a funny reminder not to take shortcuts or blindly chase trends.

That's the moral of the story: music that lasts comes from passion, authenticity and joy, not from chasing a quick buck. The burrito may never have gone viral, but the lesson was worth every pound spent.

For any young musician or creator reading this, take heed: don't chase the quick buck. Craft a story, create a message. Play the long game. Get a team that can make it happen. Build a story worth telling, not just a spectacle for the sake of attention. Ultimately, if your creation isn't authentic, it will crumble, no matter how many talented people you bring on board or how much money you throw at it. By all means roll your burritos, but do it for the love of the food, not the fame!

Conclusion

There's a hell of a lot to remember and a hell of a lot going on in the music industry, and loads of stuff came up for me while I was writing this book. In particular, I remember the friends who have tragically lost their lives to depression, and those who have lost their passion for music through getting caught up in the many pitfalls of the industry. Writing this has also made me think back to all the wild times, the laughs, the breathtaking moments of adrenaline, and that reminds me why I'm still doing what I do.

The music industry is a bizarre business, but there's truly nothing like it in the world. I genuinely hope this book has made you re-evaluate some (or all) of your approach. I trust it has also answered some important questions and made you ask many more.

It's my desire to help you realise your dreams without the hazards that so many can fall prey to down that long road.

I wish you the best in your music career. Your passion and dedication can lead you to a rewarding career in music. Thank you for joining me on mine, and always remember, your music has the power to change lives, including your own.

Say Hello

I never turn down the opportunity to link up with other artists, and I'd love to make that connection with you. Write to me @hellohughzy, join my mailing list, come to my gigs, join my hangouts online and check out my podcast. Tell me your story – I'd sincerely love to hear from you and talk about the journey you've been on. Of course, if I can also help you to progress your music career, and if you would like to work together on a specific project, my team and I at Cherry Up Projects would love to be of assistance, no matter what stage of your career you're at – whether you already have a record deal or you're starting out and trying to get people to take notice. We'd love you to join the family.

If you'd like to hear my music, see what else I'm up to, please visit my website, www.hughzy.com and get in touch.

Alternatively, visit www.cherryupprojects.com if you would like help with any of the following:

- Management
- Honing your message
- Building your brand
- Learning more about the recording process
- Learning about cost vs time vs direction
- Bringing your musical ideas to life
- Growing your community
- Creating a team
- Implementing a campaign
- Building a brand

Notes

1 J Graham, 'Tommy Emmanuel Interview', *Guitar Interactive* (14 September 2020), https://guitarinteractivemagazine.com/features/tommy-emmanuel, accessed 10 June 2025
2 M Anderson et al, 'Connection, Creativity and Drama: Teen life on social media in 2022' (Pew Research Centre, 16 November 2022), www.pewresearch.org/internet/2022/11/16/connection-creativity-and-drama-teen-life-on-social-media-in-2022, accessed 11 June 2025
3 Golden Steps ABA, 'Average Human Attention Span (Statistics)' (Golden Steps ABA, 4 March 2025), www.goldenstepsaba.com/resources/average-attention-span, accessed 11 June 2025

4 Backlinko, 'TikTok Statistics You Need to Know' (Backlinko, 8 March 2025), https://backlinko.com/tiktok-users, accessed 14 June 2025
5 M Yaqub, 'Average Time Spent On Social Media: The latest numbers' (BusinessDasher, 4 November 2024), www.businessdasher.com/average-time-spent-on-social-media, accessed 14 June 2025
6 New Mentalities, 'Ed Sheeran – I'm not posting selfies' (6 November 2021), www.youtube.com/watch?v=XpHvu0L_QZw&ab_channel=NewMentalities, accessed 11 August 2025
7 H Burman, *Avicii – I'm Tim* (Netflix, 2024), accessed 18 June 2025
8 KR Popper, *The Logic of Scientific Discovery* (University Press, 1959)
9 A Shering, 'Alan Watt's backwards law and 3 ways it can help with your mental health' (12 June 2018), www.brooklyntherapist.net/blog/2018/6/12/alan-watts-backwards-law, accessed 11 August 2025
10 RE Buswell and DS Lopez, 'wuxin. (mushin; musim)', *The Princeton Dictionary of Buddhism* (2014), www.oxfordreference.com/display/10.1093/acref/9780190681159.001.0001/acref-9780190681159-e-5005, accessed 11 August 2025

Acknowledgements

Everything in this book is based on a lifetime of experiences, with countless individuals who all deserve my gratitude. That said, here are a few special mentions that I feel deserve particular acknowledgement.

This book was possible thanks to my dear friend Chris Arnold and the team at Made Impact. I'm eternally grateful for their support in bringing this project to life. Made Impact is a global initiative for peace, amplifying the power of international exchange by collecting one million stories to showcase its transformative impact.

To Mads, Emma, Mum, Dave, Dad, Polly, Cleo, Josh and Jen – I couldn't have done this without you, and you'll always keep me firmly on the ground.

To Rob and everyone at Fuj Records, Absolute Music, and Bucks Music Group, and to Neil O'Brien and Ross, Simon Duffy at Tri-Tone and Richard Acosta at INS – I'm truly grateful for our collaboration together in recent years. Long may it continue.

To my friend and editor Jacqueline Burns, for your help and for those long lengthy, philosophical business and nonsense chats!

To Richard and Vicky Turvey, Tom and Jess Longworth, Tom Speight, Rob and Claire Hack, Mike and Evelyn Halls, for your continued love and friendship. You're the funniest, most understanding, cleverest and craziest characters, whose stories could fill ten books on their own.

To my students and developing road warriors; I have your back. Thanks for making the journey so fun. Special mentions to Mali Anthony and Dom Samagaio – I'm so proud of all you've accomplished.

To special collaborators and mastermind groups over the years. To James Scroggs for your friendship and honesty, and for teaching me the value of being a trailblazer and not waiting for approval. To Bernie Hollywood OBE JP and the Boat of Hope team.

To Paul Walsham, Callum Williams, Tom Atkinson, Norman Higham, Tom Green, Marcel Hunziker, Callum McMorran, Chris Howard, Ally McDonald,

ACKNOWLEDGEMENTS

Thom Morecroft, John Bird Jnr, Gerry Morgan, Gareth Lang, Dan Dare, Ryan Keen, Georgia Derrick, Maria Jordan, Sam and Dave Heyes, and all my other fellow road warriors out there, probably right now on some bus going through the jungle on the far side of the world.

Special thanks to all the venues I've performed at and had great times in. Special mentions to Terrence at The Kirkfield, Carl at The Avenue, John at Hampsons Bar and Emily at The Venue.

A particular special thank you to all the maniacs, chancers, hopefuls, dreamers, doers, celebrities, superstars, performers, writers, producers, managers, labels, agents and everyone else, for your amazing stories and for letting me be a part of your journeys.

Thank you to everyone who has appeared on the *More in the Moni* podcast and who agreed to be quoted in the book.

Finally, an extra-special thank you to Luna the cat, for your tech support.

The Author

Ben Hughes, also known by his stage name Hughzy, is a musician from Liverpool, UK. His multi-faceted and impressive career has taken him worldwide, including sharing the stage with iconic artists like Fleetwood Mac, RFM, Tommy Emmanuel CGP and Mel C. Praised by the late Brian Clifford, former BBC Director of Corporate Promotions, as one of the most influential figures he's met, Ben is known for his exceptional energy, talent, creativity and ability to network.

Ben has worked as a writer, artist developer and session musician for many years at renowned studios like Parr Street and Kempston Street Studios in Liverpool. In

2021, after years of touring and consulting, Ben launched Cherry Up Projects, a company specialising in artist and personal brand development, that helps to build artist and influencer careers internationally. Ben personally oversees the development process of each campaign.

Ben is passionate about charity and education, having taught at various university institutions in the UK. He was the musical director for the Boat of Hope campaign, which in 2021 raised awareness of mental health issues to a global audience.

In addition to his performance career, Ben is the host of the podcast *More in the Moni*, where he interviews industry legends on various aspects of their careers, with the goal of informing aspirational talents about the music industry. His expertise has also led him to speak at TEDx and at numerous festivals and industry events.

- www.hughzy.com
- www.facebook.com/hellohughzy
- @hellohughzy
- @hellohughzy
- @hellohughzy